STITCH IT SIMPLE

STITCH IT SIMPLE

25 hand sewn projects to make and share

Beth Sheard

photography by Steven Wooster

The Taunton Press

The Taunton Press
Inspiration for hands-on living®

The Taunton Press, Inc., 63 South Main Street,
PO Box 5506, Newtown, CT 06470-5506
email: tp@taunton.com

© Berry & Bridges Ltd. 2014

Text and project designs © Beth Sheard 2014

UK edition published in 2014 by
Berry & Bridges Ltd.
Belsize Business Center
258 Belsize Road
London NW6 4BT

Designer: Anne Wilson
Editor: Katie Hardwicke
Styling: Susan Berry
Illustrations: Beth Sheard

Library of Congress Cataloging-in-Publication Data
in progress
ISBN 978-1-62710-759-4

Reproduced in UK
Printed in China

CONTENTS

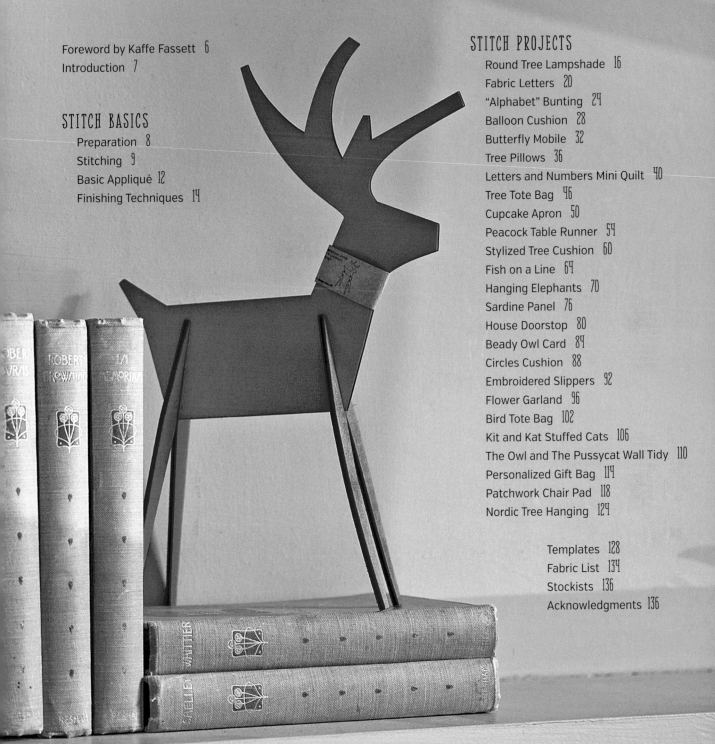

FOREWORD BY KAFFE FASSETT

It is with a sense of great pride that I write this foreword, for a budding designer that I've seen grow from such a tiny child. Stephen Sheard, Beth's father, was the first yarn manufacturer to see my work when I started knitting back in the 70s. His company, Rowan, supplied the yarn for my first book *Glorious Knitting*, and we worked together till his retirement in 2008.

I watched Beth grow up on the rugged hills of Yorkshire and became aware of her flair for design through things like her delicately collaged Christmas cards. She now assists me in the studio; organizing the million and one behind the scenes details like travel, cataloging, and storing our museum shows from around the world, and keeping track of the endless collections of knit and fabric designs being produced.

Her new book came as a bit of a shock (where did she find the time to do all that?) but, a delicious one. It is always exciting to see a fresh hand and eye using the fabric collections I have grown so used to. Beth's warm use of color should encourage many people who take pride in making their homes personal to use more color and texture in their furnishings. The ideas are simple enough for beginners to have a go and get started on the rewarding life of a maker. At the same time, more experienced sewers can use these concepts as seeds to grow their own more complex use of printed cloth in their homes.

When designing this collection of prints, I hoped it would become a paint box for others to create their own personal look, and Beth has done just that, in her confident youthful style. I look forward eagerly to see what follows from this young designer.

INTRODUCTION

I love to make small, contemporary pieces for the home or to give to friends and family as presents. I think there is nothing more special than to receive a handmade gift or card—people really treasure them, and appreciate the time, thought, and love that has gone into making them.

The projects in this book range from greeting cards to shopper "tote" bags, to a "starter" quilt, which is easy to piece together; the perfect place to start for your first quilt perhaps? There are cushions for the living room, a doorstop, slippers to keep your feet warm and looking great, a cute apron for baking, a wall tidy to hide away bits and pieces in your bedroom or office—something for every room and every occasion.

While the projects are straightforward and easy to follow if you are new to sewing, they are also sure to appeal to the more experienced sewer, with lots of possibilities for adapting the ideas to make your own.

Creating great textile projects doesn't have to be complicated or time consuming. It is all about choosing the right fabrics and using them in a simple and effective way to create something that is both striking to look at, and practical to use in everyday life.

This is what is so fantastic about the Kaffe Fassett Collective fabrics range—every pattern has so many possibilities and such a diverse range of uses. The huge choice of colorways means that you can substitute one color for another, to create an entirely different feel and mood. You may want to make the projects in this book exactly as they appear, or put your own flair and color choices into them.

I hope this book provides you with the ideas and inspiration to explore color and pattern—and that making these projects gives you as much pleasure as I had creating them. And remember, every time you make a handmade project, it is truly individual to you. No one will have one exactly the same! Make it, use it, and be proud to show it off and say "I made that!"

STITCH BASICS

PREPARATION

Before you start a project, find a comfortable place to work with a large enough table to lay out your fabric, and set up an ironing board nearby. It pays to work in good light, either in front of a window or with directed light from a lamp.

If you are using a sewing machine, thread it with appropriate thread. If hand sewing, make sure you have all your hand stitching equipment nearby.

BASIC KIT

- Sewing machine
- Ironing board and iron
- Long-handled dressmaker's shears
- Embroidery scissors
- Tape measure/ruler
- Pins
- Selection of needles, such as sewing needles, embroidery needles, yarn needles
- Fading fabric marker or water-soluble pen
- Sewing threads and embroidery floss
- Tapestry yarn
- Fusible web, such as Bondaweb or HeatnBond

CUTTING OUT FABRIC

It is important when cutting out fabric to work with the straight grain (unless stated otherwise), as all fabrics are woven with threads running vertically and horizontally. Your cut edges should align with these threads—if you cut following the selvage edge then you will achieve a neat, straight line. On a printed fabric, it is fairly easy to see if the pattern is straight.

- It is usually a good idea to press your fabric first before cutting out to make sure it is even and straight.

- Use a sharp pair of long-handled dressmaker's shears to cut larger pieces of fabric. Very small pieces, or tricky shapes, can be cut with small fabric or embroidery scissors.

- Never use fabric scissors to cut paper as it blunts the blade.

> BETH'S TIP
> In some projects you may prefer to baste (tack) your fabric together before machine sewing. Simply take long running stitches to temporarily join the pieces, then remove the stitches once sewn. Use bright thread so that your stitches are visible.

STITCHING

The projects in this book use either machine or hand stitching, or sometimes both. Machine stitching is the easiest option when joining larger pieces of fabric together but hand sewing is ideal for small or tricky items, or to add decorative effects and appliqué.

STITCHING SEAMS

The most efficient way to join two fabrics together is with a line of straight stitching (creating a seam), either on the machine or by hand with backstitches (see right). Make sure that the stitching is close enough and strong enough to prevent the fabrics from pulling apart.

❀ Always allow a little extra fabric when creating seams to avoid the fabric fraying. The standard seam allowance is approximately ⅜in/1cm, unless otherwise stated.

❀ Start and finish a line of machine stitches with a few backstitches, using the reverse stitch option; this helps prevent the stitches from unraveling.

BASIC HAND STITCHING

When hand stitching, make sure you are using the right needle and thread for the job. Hand stitching cotton fabric is best done with cotton sewing thread and a standard sewing needle (known as a sharp). Decorative stitches are best done with embroidery floss or even yarn or tapestry yarn, and using an appropriate embroidery needle or yarn needle.

Start a line of hand stitches by threading the needle and oversewing the first stitch or two to secure them. Finish by similarly oversewing the last couple of stitches, to prevent them unraveling. Trim any ends.

BACKSTITCH

This stitch is mainly used for sewing two fabrics together as it creates a continuous line of stitching that is very strong.

Bring your needle to the front at 1 (a stitch length from where you want to start the line of stitching), then take a short backward stitch down at 2. Bring the needle up to the front at 3, then back down at 1. Keep working backward and forward to form a continuous line.

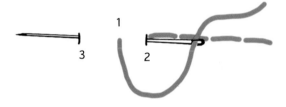

OVERSEWING OR SLIP STITCH

This is useful for closing up gaps left in seams after stuffing. Using a matching thread and a sewing needle, take small stitches as shown.

Bring the needle through one piece of fabric at the edge of the gap, take it across to the other side, and make a small stitch, then pull the thread to join the two sides. Keep stitching until the gap is closed.

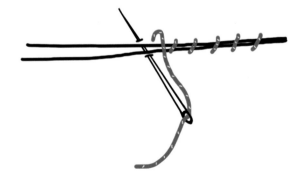

DECORATIVE STITCHES

There are many different decorative stitches to choose from but I have used a small selection for the projects.

RUNNING STITCH

Running stitch is an easy, versatile, decorative stitch.

Working from left to right, make small even stitches. The stitch should be the same length as the space between each stitch. You can alter the length of the stitch and how close together the stitches are for different effects.

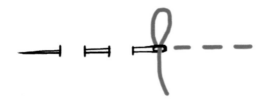

SATIN STITCH

This is a series of parallel stitches worked closely together to create a decorative surface.

Make a straight stitch across the area you would like to cover. Bring the needle up again right next to the start of the first stitch and make a second stitch the same length as the first.
Repeat to make a row of stitches, as close together as possible, until the area is filled.

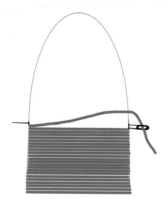

APPLIQUÉ STITCH EDGING

When using a matching thread, this stitch gives a subtle finish, or worked in a contrasting thread it creates a lovely decorative edge.

Working around your appliqué shape, work evenly sized and spaced straight stitches at right angles to the edge of the fabric shape.

CROSS STITCH

Cross stitches can be used singly, as an eye for example, or in groups, or in a line for decoration along an edge.

To make a single cross stitch, make a diagonal stitch sloping from top left **(1)** to bottom right **(2)**.
Bring the needle up again at bottom left **(3)** to top right **(4)** to make another diagonal stitch in the opposite direction, over the first.
When stitching a line of cross stitches, work all the bottom stitches first, spacing them evenly, then the top stitches.

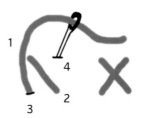

BLANKET STITCH

Blanket stitch is ideal to use to finish a fabric's edge to prevent fraying and to add decoration.

Push the needle through from the back to the front, coming out about ⅜in/1cm in from the edge of the fabric (A).

Anchor the first stitch by bringing the needle back up at the same spot where you started (1), creating a loop around the edge, take the needle under the loop you just created (B). This secures your thread so you are ready to sew your first blanket stitch. Push the needle through to the back of the fabric about ⅜in/1cm along from the anchored stitch. Take the needle through the loop of thread and pull tight (C). Make sure your thread is through the loop.

Repeat steps A–C to form continuous, evenly spaced blanket stitches (D).

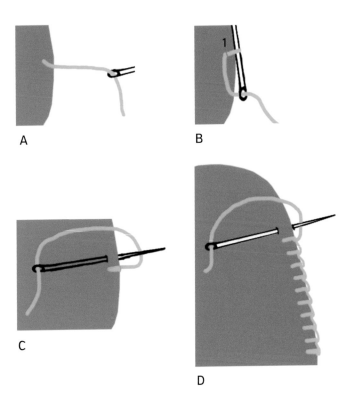

A
B
C
D

FRENCH KNOTS

These are great for adding detail and creating a 3-D effect.

Push the needle through to the front in the place you want your knot. Hold the needle with your needle hand and keep the thread taut with your other hand (A).

Place the needle in front of the stretched thread. This will make the next step easier, and will prevent the knot from looking wonky later on (B). Wrap the thread around the needle 3 or 4 times, holding the wraps in place with the finger of your other hand (C). Keep your non-needle hand taut. Give the thread a little downward tug, so that the coil will tighten up, and slide it down your needle to make a little bundle against the fabric.

With the coil snugly held in position against the surface, insert the tip of your needle just next to (but not into the same hole) where your thread is coming out of the fabric (D). Push the needle all the way through.

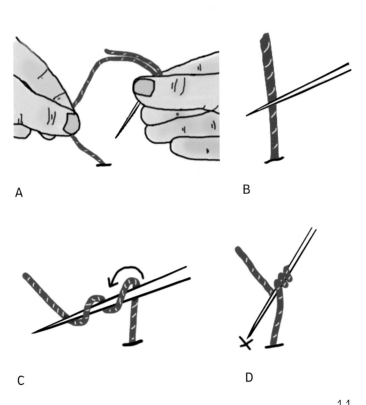

A
B
C
D

BASIC APPLIQUÉ

Appliqué is a technique for attaching a fabric shape to a background or base fabric, by sticking or stitching it in place, or both. I use an adhesive-backed paper or fusible web, such as HeatnBond or Bondaweb, to stick fabric shapes in place and then add decorative stitching around the edge to secure them and add detail.

✤ When applying one fabric to another, make sure that your fabrics are compatible—it is much easier to bond cotton to cotton, for example.

✤ If the project is washable, it is a good idea to stitch as well as stick the fabrics together, as the glue involved in sticking will wash away eventually.

✤ Stitching around the edges of an appliqué shape (by hand or machine) also helps to prevent any fraying on vulnerable fabrics.

MAKING TEMPLATES

Many of the projects in this book use special templates (see pages 128–33). All the templates need enlarging by 200% to make them actual size. Use a photocopier or scanner to enlarge the template onto a sheet of plain paper, then cut out the shape. You can, of course, reduce or enlarge the shapes to your chosen size, too.

Pin the paper template to the wrong side of your fabric or the paper backing of fusible web, flipping the template if necessary so that it looks back to front—this is especially important for letters and numbers. Once cut out, the shape will be the correct way round. Either cut out around the template, or draw around it using a fading fabric marker or water-soluble pen to create an identical fabric shape, then cut out.
If you are using several template pieces of fabric, keep them together and label them if necessary.

APPLIQUÉ STITCHES

Appliqué shapes often benefit from being stitched around the edges, either with machine or hand stitching (see page 10), which helps to secure them to the base fabric and add a decorative touch.
If machine stitching, zig-zag stitch is the most effective and easy to do. Position the fabric to be stitched so that the edge is between the feed dogs of the presser foot, set the machine to zig-zag stitch, and use this as the guide when stitching. You can create quite different looks by changing the length and width of the zig-zag.
When hand stitching, decorative stitches, such as blanket stitch (see page 11), add a pretty edge.

BETH'S TIP
Most embroidery floss is stranded, usually with six thin strands. I tend to use three strands of the floss together when embroidering, unless otherwise stated. You will need to separate the strands.

USING FUSIBLE WEB

Before cutting out the fabric shape, lay the fabric with the wrong side facing up on your ironing board. Cut a piece of fusible web slightly smaller than your fabric piece and position it on the wrong side of the fabric. Then apply heat (see tip, right) to the paper side of the fusible web to fuse it to the fabric, following the manufacturer's instructions **(A)**.

Once cooled, lay or pin your template onto the paper side of the fusible web and draw around the shape **(B)**. Remove the template and cut out the bonded fabric shape around the drawn line **(C)**. The shape is now ready to appliqué to the base fabric.

Peel the paper backing away from the shape. The glue will have transferred to the wrong side of the fabric. Simply lay the appliqué fabric shape, with the glued side down, on the right side of the base fabric, in the correct position. Check the positioning before ironing in place, following the manufacturer's instructions **(D)**.

```
IRONING FUSIBLE WEB
Using a medium hot iron, simply
press the iron down on the paper
side of the fusible web or
on the non-sticky side of the
treated appliqué fabric. Don't
rub or move the iron over the
surface as you may inadvertently
spread the glue beyond the edges
of the fabric.
```

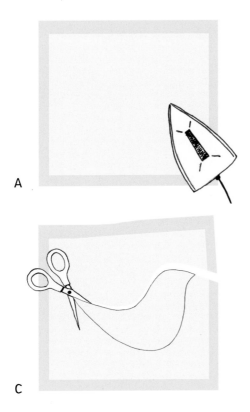

A

B

C

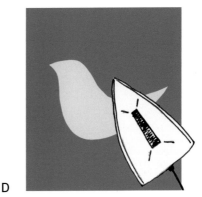

D

FINISHING TECHNIQUES

FINISHING A CUSHION—ENVELOPE BACK

Cut two pieces from your backing fabric, measuring the height of your cushion, including seam allowances, and about three-quarters of the width, adding an extra 2in/5cm on the width. On the short, right edge of one piece of fabric, fold over about ⅝in/1.5cm to the wrong side, press then fold again by 1¼in/3cm to make a double hem. Machine stitch in place, ¼in/5mm in from the fold. Repeat for the short left edge of the second piece **(A)**.

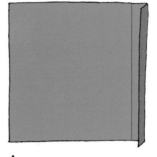
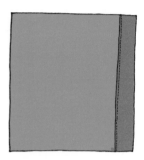

A

Lay your finished cushion front right side up on your work surface, position one backing piece on top, right side facing down, with the right folded edge facing the middle and the raw edges aligned. Place the second piece on top, right side down, overlapping the first, with the folded left edge facing the middle. Pin in place **(B)**.

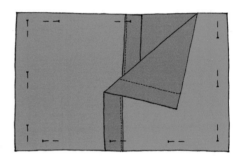

B

Keeping everything flat and all edges aligned, machine-sew around all four sides, taking a ⅜in/1cm seam, stitching over the overlapping folds of the back pieces **(C)**. Trim the corners and turn the cover right side out through the envelope fold.

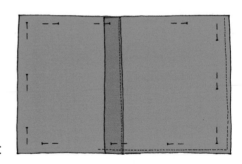

C

BETH'S TIP
Putting your cushion in and out of your cover will pull on the edges of the envelope: make a few extra stitches over the join to secure the back panels at the edges.

BINDING EDGES

Press each binding strip in half, lengthwise, wrong sides together. With the back or wrong side of your project facing up, start with the top edge. Pin the first binding strip to the backing, with the right sides together and the raw edges aligned. Sew a ⅜in/1cm seam in from the edge **(A)**. Remove the pins. Fold the strip over to the right side or front of your project and pin. Sew the binding in place a fraction of an inch away from the folded edge, enclosing all the raw edges **(B)**. This line of stitching will be visible on the back; to avoid the stitched line, slip stitch (see page 9) by hand. Trim any excess binding. Repeat for the bottom edge of the project.

To bind the two long sides, start by pressing under ⅜in/1cm at each end of the binding strip **(C)**. Once fully sewn this will enclose all the raw edges. Repeat to bind the side edges.

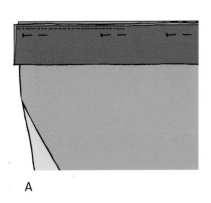

A

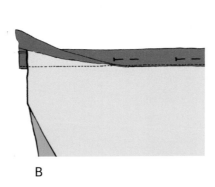

B

C

THREADING HANGING SHAPES

Thread a length of tapestry yarn about 1yd/1m long through a long yarn needle and tie a large knot in the end. Thread on several glass or ceramic beads to weigh down your hanging **(A)**. If they fall over your knots, tie a few more and re-thread your beads.

Pull the needle through the center of your first shape **(B)**. Check that the shape hangs straight and alter the position of the thread if not. When it is balanced, pass the thread through the second and the third shapes, and so on, adjusting as you go.

Your shapes should hang by themselves on your tapestry yarn, if not, tie a knot in the thread below each shape to stop it sliding down. Finish off the thread by tying a loop for hanging.

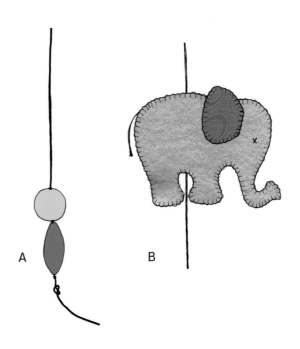

A

B

ROUND TREE LAMPSHADE

This simple project of stylized tree motifs combines circles of leaves with rectangular trunks. You can either make it for a pendant light or a table lamp, adapting it with as many or as few tree motifs to fit, and using lots of different fabric scraps. I chose fabrics that were quite different in pattern, but whose colors work really well together. This project uses a lampshade kit, but you can adapt it to fit an existing lampshade.

THINGS YOU NEED

- Tree templates on page 129
- Six patterned fabrics (see tip on page 18 and Cutting Out)
- 1¼yd/1¼m cotton calico/ cream linen fabric
- Fusible web
- Fading fabric marker pen
- Basic sewing kit
- Sewing machine
- Lampshade kit, 12in/30cm diameter
- Flame retardant spray

MAKING THE TREE LAMPSHADE

FINISHED LAMPSHADE SIZE
Height: 8¼in/21cm
Diameter: 12in/30cm

CUTTING OUT
FROM EACH PATTERNED FABRIC
Cut 1: 8 x 5in/20 x 10cm rectangle
FROM CALICO/CREAM LINEN
Cut 1: 11 x 40in/28 x 100cm rectangle
NOTE: All measurements include ⅝in/1.5cm seam
   allowance unless otherwise stated.

BETH'S TIP
For this project, I used six
different fabrics to make eight
motifs, and repeated two of
them, as the lampshade is in the
round so you don't see all of it
at once. You can mix and match
fabrics for this project to suit
your own budget or
taste, and use
eight different
patterns if
you like.

APPLYING THE MOTIFS
1. Copy the templates on page 129. Iron fusible web to the wrong side of the patterned fabric pieces. Draw around the trunk templates on the fusible web and cut them out. Draw a 3in/7.5cm diameter circle for the "leaves" on the fusible web and cut out.

2. Lay the calico or linen out flat on your work surface. Position the cut-out circles of "leaves" on the fabric and play around with the layout, until you find a placement that works for you. Lay them out evenly, with a gap of about 1½in/3.5cm between each and mark their positions with a fading fabric marker pen. Allow at least a 3in/7.5cm border along the top and 2¼in/5.5cm border at the sides.

3. Peel off the backing paper and iron the circle onto your calico. Repeat until all eight circles are ironed in place **(A)**.

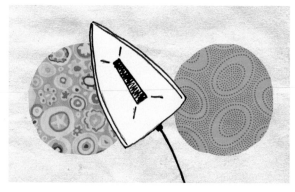

A. Ironing the "leaves" in place.

ADDING STITCH DETAILS

4. Once you've ironed the circles, select a zig-zag stitch on your sewing machine and, starting at the bottom in the middle, machine-sew all the way around the circle **(B)**. By starting at the bottom in the middle, the ends will be covered once your tree trunks are in place. Repeat to stitch all the circles. Alternatively, you could hand appliqué using blanket stitch.

5. Next, lay out the tree trunks until you are happy with the placement. Peel off the fusible web backing and iron in place, then zig-zag stitch as before. Repeat until all your trees have a trunk **(C)**.

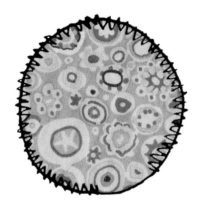

B. Zig-zag stitching around each circle.

C. Laying out the trunk patterns so that no two trunks of the same fabric are next to each other.

FINISHING THE LAMPSHADE

6. To assemble your lampshade, follow the instructions supplied with your lampshade kit. Spray with flame retardant spray. Alternatively, you could use an existing lampshade, or buy a plain one to decorate. Measure the height and circumference and add ⅝in/1.5cm for seam allowances. You will need thin double-sided sticky tape to finish the shade.

FABRIC LETTERS

Creating small, stuffed letters from bright fabrics, very simply hand stitched, gives you lots of creative opportunities! Personalize your room with your name or make a statement, with stuffed letters on your mantelpiece or shelves. You could also use numbers in the same way. I have made my letters from a bright spot fabric that comes in many different colorways, but the fabric choices are yours.

THINGS YOU NEED

* Letter templates on page 132
* Piece of spot fabric for each of your letters, approx 9½ x 8in/24 x 20cm, in complementary colors, or you can use the same color fabric for each letter
* Piece of thick wool felt, approx 9½ x 8in/ 24 x 20cm, for backing each letter
* Basic sewing kit
* Embroidery floss in coordinating colors and embroidery needle
* Batting (wadding) or fiberfill stuffing

MAKING THE FABRIC LETTERS

FINISHED LETTER SIZE
Height: 8in/20cm

CUTTING OUT
FROM SPOT FABRIC
Cut one rectangle per letter, ¾in/2cm larger all round
than your letter templates
FROM FELT
Cut one rectangle per letter, ¾in/2cm larger all round
than your letter templates
FROM BATTING (WADDING) OR STUFFING
A piece about the same size as your fabric rectangles
per letter

PREPARATION
1. Copy your chosen letter templates from page 132.
   See the tip below for cutting out holes in letters like
   "A" and "P." Pin the template to the right side of the
   spot fabric and cut out **(A)**.

2. Pin the template to the thick felt and cut out.
   If your felt has a right and wrong side, pin the
   template to the wrong side to ensure that the letter
   matches the front.

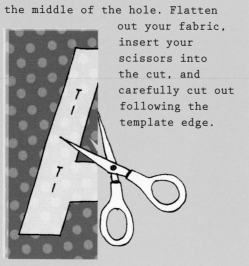

BETH'S TIP
When cutting out letters like
"A," which have tricky holes,
fold your letter in half and make
a small cut with your scissors in
the middle of the hole. Flatten
out your fabric,
insert your
scissors into
the cut, and
carefully cut out
following the
template edge.

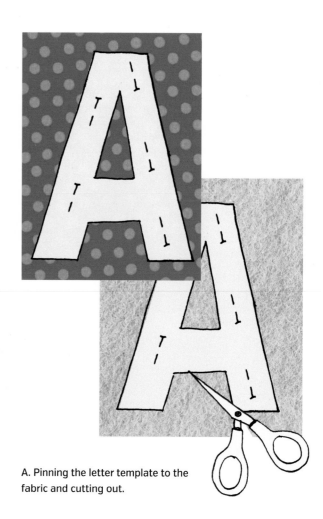

A. Pinning the letter template to the
fabric and cutting out.

SEWING THE LETTERS

3. Pin the cut-out fabric letter and felt letter, wrong sides together. Using blanket stitch (see page 11), sew the letters together, using a contrasting colored embroidery floss. Leave a gap in the seam along the top or side of your letter for inserting the stuffing (**B**). Remove the pins.

STUFFING THE LETTERS

4. Tear pieces of batting (wadding) or fiberfill so that you have lots of small balls. Stuff the letter through the gap by pushing the filling into all the corners—you can use the blunt end of a pencil or a knitting needle to help you get the stuffing all the way to the bottom and into any tricky areas (**C**).

5. Finish your letter by sewing closed the gap in the seam, using blanket stitch as before. Sew a couple of small stitches to secure the thread.

B. Blanket stitching around the edges.

C. Stuffing the letter with filling then sewing the gap closed.

"ALPHABET" BUNTING

This project may look a little daunting but don't worry, it is very easy and so effective! Use the letters to display a message—"Happy Birthday," your name, "Sophie's Room," "Congratulations"… The pennants are reversible, backed with patterned fabric that is different from the one used for the letters, so you can flip the pennants if you wish to brighten up your room all year round!

THINGS YOU NEED

- Bunting and Letter templates on pages 128 and 132
- Solid-color cream cotton, linen, or similar fabric
- Patterned cotton fabric (allow approx 9 x 9in/23 x 23cm per pennant)
- Fusible web
- Basic sewing kit
- Sewing machine and matching sewing thread
- Chunky yarn, leather thong, thick twine, or string, for hanging

MAKING THE BUNTING

PREPARATION

1. Copy the bunting template 1 on page 128 and pin it to the wrong side of the patterned fabric. Repeat with template 2 on your solid-color fabric **(A)**. Cut out the pieces, cutting enough pairs for the number of pennants you require.

2. Iron fusible web to the wrong side of the fabric for your letters. Copy the letter template, following the tips on page 22 for tricky or asymmetrical letters. Pin the template to the prepared fabric and cut out the shape.

3. Peel off the paper backing and iron your letter in place on the right side of the solid-color fabric pennant. Stitch around the edges, either by hand using backstitch or with a close zig-zag stitch on your sewing machine **(B)**.

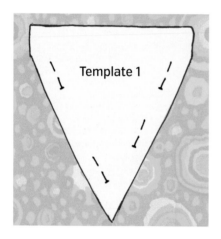

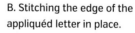

B. Stitching the edge of the appliquéd letter in place.

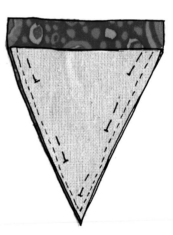

C. Pinning and sewing the solid-color and patterned pennants, with right sides together.

SEWING THE PENNANTS

4. Pin the plain and patterned pennants right sides together and then machine-sew the two longest edges as shown, taking a ⅜in/1cm seam allowance **(C)**. Clip the point off the triangle, avoiding the stitching, to give your bunting a neat, sharp tip.

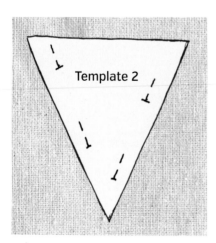

A. Pinning the templates to the wrong side of the fabric and cutting out.

5. Turn your triangle right side out and press the two long sides. On the top flap, press the side edges of the patterned fabric under at a slight angle, as shown. Press the long top edge under by ¼in/5mm **(D)**.

D. Pressing the side edges then the top edge of the flap.

6. Now fold the top fabric strip over so that the patterned fabric forms a header on the solid fabric. Machine-sew along the bottom edge, close to the fold to create a "channel" for the hanging line.

THREADING THE PENNANTS

7. To thread your letter pennants together, attach the end of your yarn, or whatever you are using, to a safety-pin. Thread the safety-pin through the channels, pushing it through, and adding the letters in reverse order. Leave about 12in/30cm at either end for tying up your bunting.

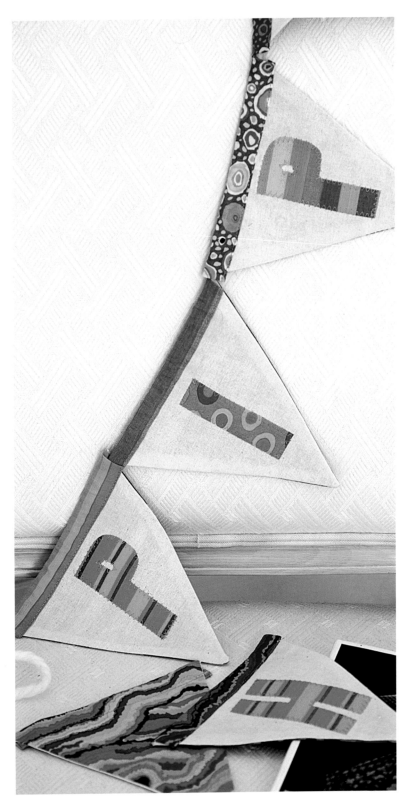

BALLOON CUSHION

This cushion has a lovely, fairground appeal to it, made up of vibrant patterns and colors. The balloon itself looks complex but is in fact made easy by simply layering the fabric pieces on top of each other. A few backstiches provide the "ropes" for the balloon itself and the elements of the balloon are defined with hand-stitched blanket stitches, too.

THINGS YOU NEED

* Hot air balloon templates on page 129
* Spot fabric (A), for cushion
* Zig-zag fabric (B), for balloon
* Floral patterned fabric (C), for balloon
* Stripe fabric (D), for basket
* Fusible web
* Embroidery floss in coordinating colors and embroidery needle
* Basic sewing kit
* Sewing machine and matching thread
* 20in/50cm square pillow form (cushion pad)

MAKING THE BALLOON CUSHION

FINISHED SIZE
20 x 20in/50 x 50cm

CUTTING OUT
FOR THE CUSHION
Fabric A, cut 1: 21in/53cm square, for front; cut 2:
  21 x 14in/53 x 36cm rectangles, for back
FOR THE BALLOON
Fabric B, cut 2: 12 x 12in/30 x 30cm squares
Fabric C, cut 2: 10 x 10in/25 x 25cm squares
FOR THE BASKET:
Fabric D, cut 1: 3¼ x 5in /8.5 x 10.5cm rectangle
Note: All measurements include ⅝in/1.5cm seam
  allowance unless otherwise stated.

BETH'S TIP
When making this cushion,
I found it best to position
the balloon first and then
add the basket, rather than
working from the bottom
of the basket upward. The
balloon is the focal point,
and the trickiest part, so
position this first. As the
basket was just a simple
rectangle I didn't need to
bond it first, but you can
if you wish. If you find it
easier, position the basket
first, and then do all
the stitching at the
same time.

CREATING THE BALLOON

1. Cut out pieces of fusible web to the dimensions of fabric B and C and iron to the wrong side of each piece of fabric. (You will then have four pieces of fabric backed with fusible web.)

2. Copy the template on page 129 four times and cut out the pieces labeled 1–4. Draw around each balloon template on the fusible web and cut out (A). Peel off the backing paper.

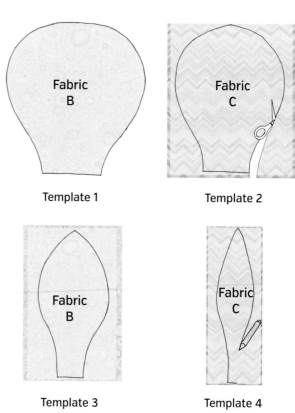

A. Preparing templates 1–4 on the bonded fabrics (B and C).

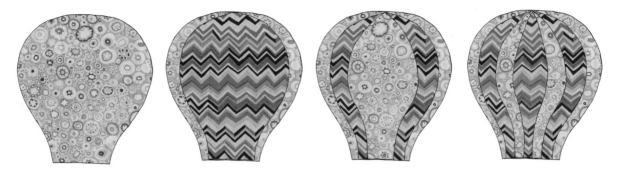

B. Positioning the fabric motifs in order, 1–4, and ironing in place.

3. In this order, position piece 1 on your backing fabric, 7in/18cm from the base, and then lay piece 2 on top of piece 1, then piece 3 on top of piece 2, and finally piece 4 on top of piece 3. Once the position looks right, iron in place **(B)**.

4. Using blanket stitch (see page 11), stitch around each of the pieces of your balloon at a time, following the edge of each separate piece of fabric **(C)**.

CREATING THE BASKET AND "ROPES"

5. Position the basket and pin or iron in place, then blanket stitch along all four edges.

6. Using backstitch, create eight evenly spaced lines of stitching, each from the bottom of the balloon to the basket, to form the "ropes" that attach the balloon to the basket **(D)**.

FINISHING THE CUSHION

7. Make up the cushion with an envelope back (see page 14) using the fabric A rectangles, then insert the pillow form (cushion pad) to finish.

C. Blanket stitching around the edge of each fabric piece.

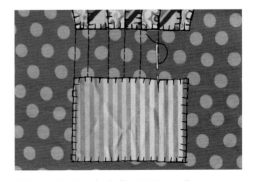

D. Backstitching the balloon's "ropes."

BUTTERFLY MOBILE

This fun mobile is really versatile—once your butterflies are threaded you can hang them from anywhere. I chose a nice, smooth branch from the garden (which you could paint, too) but they'd look just as lovely on a circular frame, or you could even make several lengths and hang them across a window. You can also make as many or as few butterflies as you like, and either use contrasting fabrics or, if you prefer, all in matching fabric.

THINGS YOU NEED

* Butterfly templates on page 129
* Approx ¼yd/¼m in each of five different patterned cotton fabrics
* Fusible web
* Skein of twine or thick colored thread or yarn
* Basic sewing kit
* Large yarn needle
* Glass or ceramic beads

MAKING THE BUTTERFLY MOBILE

FINISHED SIZE
Length: 21¾in/55cm

CUTTING OUT
FROM PATTERNED FABRIC
Cut 10: 6 x 4¾in/15 x 12cm rectangles
Cut 10: 4¾ x 4in/12 x 10cm rectangles
FROM FUSIBLE WEB
Cut 5: 6 x 4¾in/15 x 12cm rectangles (a fraction of an inch smaller than your fabric rectangles)
Cut 5: 4¾ x 4in/12 x 10cm rectangles (a fraction of an inch smaller than your fabric rectangles)

BETH'S TIP
You can place your butterflies in any number of combinations. I positioned my smaller butterflies at the top and the larger ones at the bottom. Some lengths of thread have two butterflies and some only one.

PREPARATION
1. Iron a large rectangle of fusible web onto the wrong side of your first large fabric rectangle, let cool, and peel off the backing. Iron your matching large fabric rectangle, right side up, on top of the adhesive, creating a "sandwich" of fabric/fusible web/fabric **(A)**. Let cool, keeping the fabric flat.

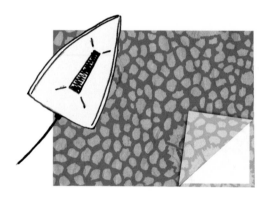

A. Creating a fabric "sandwich" with matching fabrics.

2. Repeat to combine the remaining matching rectangles of fabric so you have five large double-sided fabric rectangles and five small double-sided fabric rectangles.

MAKING THE BUTTERFLIES
3. Copy the templates on page 129 and pin to the fabric pieces. Cut out your butterflies: five large and five small.

MAKING THE MOBILE

4. Measure seven pieces of twine or thick thread, each piece 25½in/65cm long–you will trim off any excess once you have finished your mobile.

5. Lay out the lengths of twine next to each other on a flat surface. Next, lay your butterflies on top of the twine to decide roughly where you want to position them.

6. Use the twine to attach your butterflies. Thread a length of twine onto a needle and sew a butterfly to the twine with backstitch (see page 9), then sew on the next butterfly **(B)**. Use each length of twine to attach the butterflies in your chosen order and position.

7. To weigh down your butterflies, tie glass beads onto the bottom of your twine (see page 15). Trim any excess twine below the knot, and repeat until all your lengths of twine have beads attached.

HANGING THE BUTTERFLIES

8. You can hang your butterflies any way you wish: I chose a nice smooth twig. Balance your twig on a flat surface, weighting down the ends if necessary so it doesn't move while you are tying on your butterfly lengths. Tie the tops of your threads to your twig with a single knot; you'll be able to adjust the length of each thread, and then tie a couple more knots so the threads are secure. Trim off any excess thread.

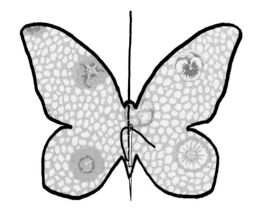

B. Sewing the butterfly to the twine using backstitch.

TREE PILLOWS

I used the same tree motif to create two versions of this little pillow: one on canvas and a bedlinen version made of softer cotton with a few more hand stitches. A stylized tree motif also appears on a longer cushion design on red cotton on page 60. The small canvas pillow here uses just three of the larger motifs and is machine stitched, and the pillowslip version has smaller trees and some additional hand stitching.

THINGS YOU NEED

- Tree template on page 128
- Solid-color cream cotton, linen, or similar fabric, for the small pillow, or
- White or cream cotton pillowslip (pillow case)
- Patterned cotton fabric, striped for your trees and spotty for your circles
- Fusible web
- Embroidery floss in coordinating colors and embroidery needle
- Basic sewing kit
- Sewing machine and matching thread
- 15¾ x 12in/40 x 30cm pillow form (cushion pad), for small pillow

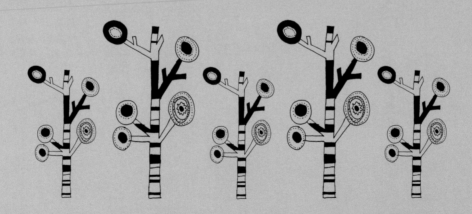

MAKING THE SMALL PILLOW

CUTTING OUT

FOR THE FRONT

From cream cotton canvas, cut 1: 16¾ x 12¾in/ 42.5 x 32.5cm rectangle

FOR THE BACK

From cream cotton canvas, cut 2: 11 x 12¾in/ 27.5 x 32.5cm rectangles

NOTE: All measurements include ⅜in/1cm seam allowances unless otherwise stated.

PREPARATION

1. Copy the tree template on page 128 to make a large template, then reduce the size to make a smaller template. Draw around the large tree twice onto the backing of fusible web, and once for the small tree. Iron the web to the wrong side of the striped fabric. Cut out around the drawn lines.

2. Iron fusible web to the wrong side of the spotty fabric. Following the pattern on the spotty fabric, cut out 15 circles or spots; 12 large and 3 small **(A)**.

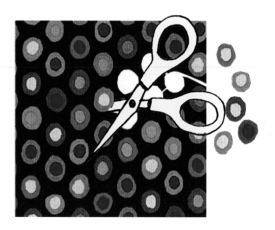

A. Cut out circles from the spotty fabric, following the pattern.

APPLYING THE TREES

3. Position the trees on the large piece of cream fabric, 4in/10cm apart and 2½in/6cm from the bottom edge. Peel off the paper backing and iron the trees in place.

4. Position the cut-out circles at the end of the branches and iron in place **(B)**. You can do the trees first, then the circles, or both at once, it is entirely up to you.

B. Position the trees and iron in place.

BETH'S TIP
If you would prefer to cut out circles from a solid-color fabric, simply draw around a round object, like a button or bobbin, and cut out along the lines. Use a fading fabric marker or chalk pencil on the reverse of the fabric.

FINISHING THE SMALL PILLOW

5. Once everything is securely in place, you are ready
   to hand embroider. Take two strands of embroidery
   floss and, using backstitch (see page 9), sew a
   fraction in from the edge, following the outline
   of your trees. Use running stitch (see page 10) to
   attach the circles, following the pattern if your
   fabric has inner rings.

6. Make up the pillow back following the instructions
   on page 14. Insert your pillow form and your pillow
   is complete.

THE PILLOWSLIP ALTERNATIVE

As an alternative to making a cushion, use an existing
pillowslip and embroider onto it. This is a super way
of updating an old pillowslip or jazzing up a plain one.
I have used a cream pillowslip, but this project would
also look lovely on candy stripes, too.

1. Following steps 1–3 opposite, trace and cut out
   four large trees. Cut out 20 circles from the bonded
   spotty fabric.

2. Position the trees on the open end of the pillowslip,
   evenly spaced and 2¾in/6.5cm from the edge.
   Peel off the paper backing and iron your trees in
   place. Position the cut-out circles at the end of the
   branches and iron in place.

3. Either using the free-motion embroidery foot
   on your sewing machine, or hand-stitching with
   running stitch, sew the trees in place around their
   outlines, just in from the edge, taking care not to
   sew through to the back of the pillowslip.

4. Following the instructions in step 5 above, sew the
   circles in place with running stitch. Position individual
   circles between the trees, iron in place, and then sew
   a line of running stitch beneath the trees and up to
   the circles using six strands of embroidery floss (A).

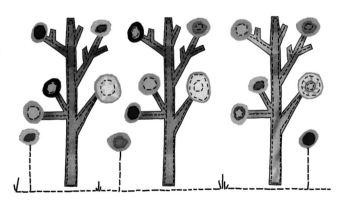

A. Sewing running stitch beneath the trees and up to
the single circles between them.

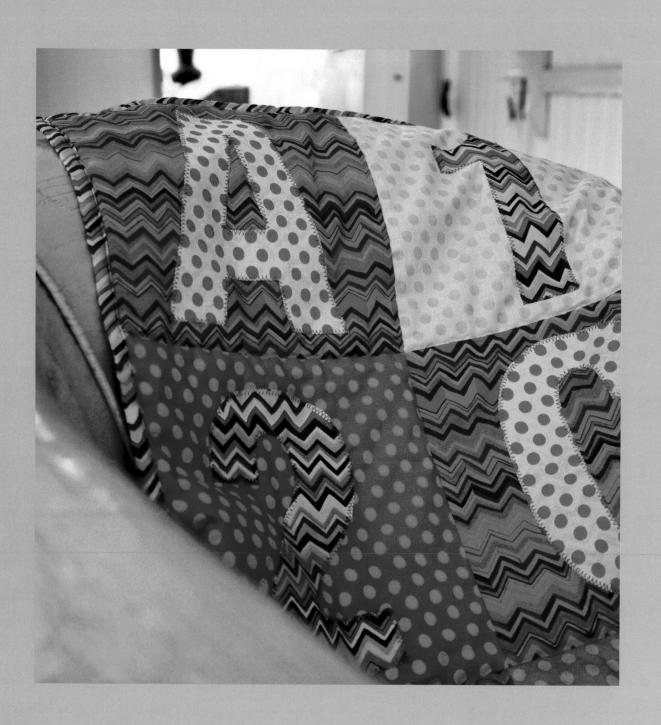

LETTERS AND NUMBERS MINI QUILT

This graphic letters and numbers mini quilt in striking brightly patterned spots and stripes, doubles up as a wonderful crib quilt or chair or sofa throw. You could customize it with letters or numbers of your choice rather than following the design shown here, which is made of up of 12 squares (three squares per row; four rows in total), with a contrasting binding and backing.

THINGS YOU NEED

* Letter and Number templates on pages 132 and 133
* Selection of coordinating patterned fabrics, approx 12in/30cm square of each
* Fusible web
* Basic sewing kit
* Sewing machine and matching thread
* 1½yd/1¼m batting (wadding)
* 1½yd/1¼m backing fabric

MAKING THE MINI QUILT

FINISHED SIZE
30 x 39in/76 x 99cm

CUTTING OUT
FOR EACH LETTER OR NUMBER (12 IN TOTAL)
Cut 1: 6¼ x 8¾in/16 x 22cm
FOR EACH QUILT SQUARE (12 IN TOTAL)
Cut 1: 11 x 10¼in/28 x 26cm
FOR BINDING
Cut 2 short strips: 2 x 31½in/5 x 80cm
Cut 2 long strips: 2 x 41¼in/5 x 105cm
NOTE: All measurements include ⅜in/1cm seam
   allowance unless otherwise stated.

PREPARATION
1. Cut out rectangles of fusible web slightly smaller
   than the fabric pieces for the letters and numbers
   and iron onto the wrong side of the fabric pieces.

2. Copy the templates for the numbers and letters
   from pages 132 and 133. Position the template on
   the web and draw around it. Remember to reverse
   the templates so your numbers and letters are
   back to front. Cut out the numbers and letters.

ATTACHING THE MOTIFS
3. Peel off the web backing and iron each fabric letter
   and number onto the middle of a fabric square.

4. Using zig-zag stitch, machine-sew around the
   outline of each letter and number to complete
   the 12 squares of your design **(A)**. Alternatively,
   appliqué stitch or blanket stitch the motifs by hand
   (see pages 10 and 11).

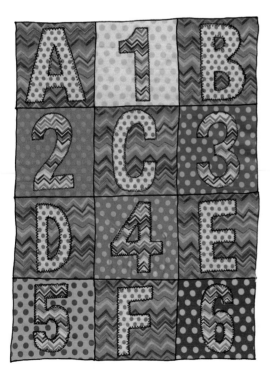

A. Zig-zag stitching the motifs in place.

SEWING THE QUILT TOP

5. Start in the top left-hand corner of your design. Take two squares, pin them right sides together and, taking a ⅜in/1cm seam allowance, sew together along the left side.

6. Take your next piece from the top row and repeat step 5. You will end up with 3 squares sewn together in a row **(B)**. Press all your seams in the same direction. Repeat this for the next three rows of squares until you have four rows of three squares sewn together.

7. Once the pieces are sewn together in separate rows, you need to sew them all together. With right sides together, position the second row upside down on top of the first. Pin, then sew them together along the bottom edge, taking a ⅜in/1cm seam **(C)**. Repeat to attach the remaining three rows in order. Press the seams flat in the same direction.

ASSEMBLING THE QUILT

8. Measure the quilt top, add 2in (5cm) to all sides and cut the backing fabric and batting to this measurement.

9. Spread out the backing fabric on a flat surface, right side down, and smooth out any creases. Put the batting on top. Lay the quilt top over the batting, right side up, and centered. Smooth out the sandwiched layers **(D)**.

B. Completing the first row.

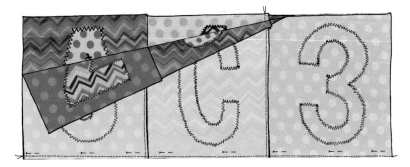

C. Sewing the rows together.

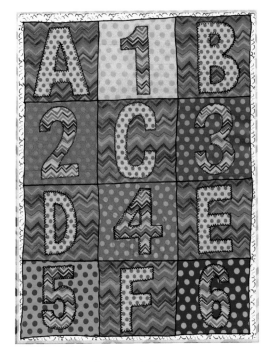

D. Making the quilt "sandwich."

E. Stitching the the quilt squares.

10. Pin all three layers together. Start with the horizontal and vertical seam lines, then pin down the middle of each square. Next, put rows of pins in diagonally. Flatten out any wrinkles.

11. Using matching thread, hand stitch in running stitch (see page 10) or machine stitch along the seam lines (horizontally first, then vertically) to hold the layers of the quilt together **(E)**.

12. Baste along the side edges to hold them together, then trim off the surplus batting and backing fabric, in line with the quilt top **(F)**.

FINISHING THE QUILT

13. Press the binding strips in half, lengthwise. With the quilt backing uppermost, pin one shorter border strip to the top edge, right sides together **(G)**. Follow the instructions on page 15 for binding the edges of the quilt.

F. Trimming the backing and batting.

G. Adding the binding.

STITCH IT SIMPLE

TREE TOTE BAG

This pretty tree design will liven up a plain cotton tote bag in no time. It uses a simple combination of solid and patterned fabrics—choose a brightly patterned spot fabric to use for the circles of "blossom" scattered over the tree, cutting around the printed shapes to give you instant embellishments.

THINGS YOU NEED

- A solid-color cotton tote bag: I used a cream bag, but you can choose any color that will complement your fabrics
- Tree template on page 131
- Orange fabric for the tree, approx 12 x 12in/30 x 30cm
- Patterned fabric for the tree trunk, approx ¼yd/¼m
- Scraps of spotty fabric for the flowers
- Fusible web
- Embroidery floss in coordinating colors and embroidery needle
- Basic sewing kit
- Sewing machine and contrasting thread

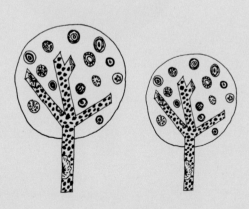

MAKING THE BAG

FINISHED SIZE
16¼ x 14½in/41.5cm x 37cm
(including handles: 27½ x 14½in/70 x 37cm)

CUTTING OUT
FROM ORANGE FABRIC
Cut 1: 9¼in/23.5cm diameter circle
FROM PATTERNED FABRIC
Cut 1: 8 x 12in/20 x 30cm rectangle

PREPARATION
1. Copy the tree template on page 131. Cut pieces of fusible web slightly smaller than your fabric pieces and iron onto the wrong side of the fabric. Trace around the tree trunk template onto the fusible web, reversing the shape. Cut out.

ADDING THE MOTIFS
2. Lay the circle of fabric on the bag, about 4¼in/11cm from the base, and roughly in the center. Iron in place **(A)**.

3. Machine stitch the circle around the edge, using a zig-zag stitch in a contrasting colored thread, and taking care not to sew through to the back of the bag.

4. Repeat steps 2 and 3 to attach the tree trunk on top of the circle, either machine stitching around the edge, or hand stitching with blanket stitch (see page 11), if you prefer **(B)**.

5. Iron a piece of fusible web onto the back of your spotty fabric. Cut out about 20 circles or spots following the pattern.

6. Peel off the backing from the circles and position them on your tree circle, a little like apples or blossom. Iron the circles in place and either machine stitch or hand stitch to finish.

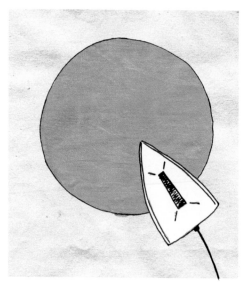

A. Ironing the circle to the bag.

B. Adding zig-zag stitching around the motifs.

CUPCAKE APRON

This design gives you a chance to show off your embroidery prowess! I created a cupcake motif for this pinafore apron, cutting out the basic cupcake shape from one fabric, and then using two different solid fabrics for the case and the topping. I used a variety of hand stitches to decorate both the cupcake and the apron itself. You can amend your decorative details to suit the shape of your apron.

THINGS YOU NEED

* Cupcake templates on page 130
* Solid-color cotton or linen apron
* Felt for the cake, 6in/15cm square
* Solid-color fabric for the frosting, approx 3½ x 4¾in/ 9 x 12cm
* Patterned fabric for the cupcake liner, approx 5 x 4¾in/13 x 12cm
* Fusible web
* Fabric glue or white (PVA) glue
* Embroidery floss and embroidery needle
* Fading fabric marker or water-soluble pen
* Tapestry yarn in two colors
* Large-eyed yarn needle

MAKING THE APRON

PREPARATION

1. Copy the cupcake templates on page 130. Cut out the cupcake shape from the cream felt, the frosting shape from the solid fabric, and the cupcake liner from the patterned fabric.

2. Iron fusible web onto the wrong side of the frosting and cupcake liner fabric pieces, draw around the templates, and cut out the shapes.

A. Ironing the frosting and liner in place on the felt cupcake shape.

STITCHING THE CUPCAKE

3. Using a small amount of fabric glue, stick the felt "cake" part of your cupcake to the apron—you can center it on the bib, as I have done, or place it on one side of the "skirt."

4. Remove the fusible web backing paper. Position the solid-color "frosting" and patterned fabric liner pieces on top of the cake and iron in place **(A)**.

5. Using a contrasting color of embroidery floss, blanket stitch (see page 11) around the edges of the cupcake liner and the frosting **(B)**.

B. Blanket stitching around the shapes.

6. To create the folded effect of the cupcake liner, sew lines of evenly spaced running stitch (see page 10) vertically down the fabric.

7. "Decorate" your frosting by sewing about 12 French knots (see page 11) at equal intervals, using a contrasting color floss if you like **(C)**, or multicolored knots for a pretty "sprinkles" effect.

C. Adding French knots and running stitches.

DECORATIVE DETAILS

You can add further decoration with some woolen embroidery. For example, embroider wording over the cupcake using backstitch and decorate the pocket with a mixture of simple running and cross stitches.

8. To create the lettering, trace out your chosen words—I used "YUM YUM"—onto the apron with a fading fabric marker or water-soluble pen.

9. Using tapestry yarn and the large-eyed needle, backstitch (see page 9) along the lines you have just drawn. Sew the letters in one color thread, then repeat next to the stitching in a second color.

10. Using a fading fabric marker, draw vertical lines approx 1in/2.5cm apart on your apron's pocket. If your pocket is shaped, like mine, start in the center and work out to the edge, creating shorter lines as you do so.

11. Work a line of running stitches along the lines, changing color every other row, and then work cross stitches in the same color over the running stitches.

PEACOCK TABLE RUNNER

It is fun to jazz up a regular table (particularly one found in a thrift store with a less-than-perfect surface) with a really striking table runner. The runner length can be altered to suit the table size as can the positioning of the motifs. On a longer runner, it would look good with a motif positioned at each end (so that it covers the fabric that drops over the edge of the table) and with just one other motif in the center.

THINGS YOU NEED

- Peacock templates on page 130
- ½yd/½m solid-color fabric for background
- ½yd/½m backing fabric
- 1yd/1m patterned fabric for border
- Fabric for birds in three different patterns or colors (A, B, C)
- Fusible web
- Sewing machine and contrasting thread
- Embroidery floss in a contrasting color and embroidery needle
- Basic sewing kit

MAKING THE RUNNER

FINISHED SIZE
41 x 15¼in/104 x 39cm

CUTTING OUT
FROM BACKGROUND FABRIC
Cut 1: 41¼ x 15¼in/105 x 39cm rectangle
FROM BACKING FABRIC
Cut 1: 41¼ x 15¼in/105 x 39cm rectangle
FROM BORDER FABRIC
Cut 2: 41¼ x 15¾in/105 x 40cm rectangles
Cut 2: 15¾ x 4in/40 x 10cm rectangles
FROM YELLOW FABRIC (A) PER BIRD
Cut 4: 4 x 6¾in/10 x 17cm rectangles
FROM RED PRINT FABRIC (B) PER BIRD
Cut 4: 4¼ x 4⅛in/11 x 10.5cm rectangles
FROM YELLOW PRINT FABRIC (C) PER BIRD
Cut 3: 3 x 4⅛in/7.5 x 10.5cm rectangles

BETH'S TIP
You will need to work out how
many birds to put on your runner,
depending on the length of
your table, so that they can be
spaced evenly along it. The one
I made had four birds on it (see
schematic right) and I turned
the motifs around so that each
faced in a different direction.
Consider making a longer one that
drops down below the edge of the
table at each end, with a bird on
each flap.

PREPARATION

1. Copy the templates on page 130. Cut pieces of fusible web slightly smaller than the fabric pieces for the birds, and iron to the wrong side of the fabric. Draw around your templates: 4 birds on fabric A, 16 feathers and wings from fabric B, 12 feathers from fabric C. Reverse two of your birds when drawing the body. Cut out the shapes.

2. Place all the cut out fabric pieces onto your background fabric. Position the first bird centered on the width, about 6in/15cm from the bottom edge. Leave approximately 10in/25cm between each peacock. Position the feathers and wings.

3. Peel off the fusbile web backing and iron the birds' bodies, feathers, and wings in position **(A)**.

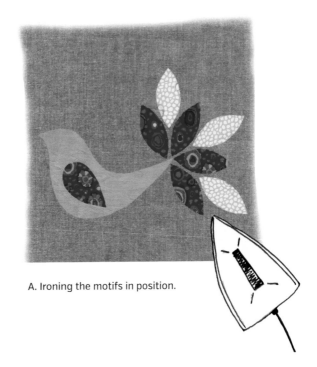

A. Ironing the motifs in position.

STITCHING THE DETAILS

4. Select zig-zag stitch on your sewing machine and sew around all the pieces of your peacock to secure them and add a pretty finish.

5. Using contrasting embroidery floss, backstitch (see page 9) three lines of stitching for the peacock's plumage. For extra detail, sew a French knot (see page 11) at the top of each line of stitching. Using the same thread, give your bird an eye. Backstitch two legs and feet beneath the body **(B)**.

6. Repeat steps 4 and 5 to complete the remaining birds.

B. Zig-zag stitching around all the pieces and adding hand embroidery details.

ADDING THE BACKING AND BORDERS

7. Lay out the backing fabric, right side down. Lay your peacock runner on top, right side up. Then position your two long border pieces along the long edges, with right sides facing. Pin all the layers together and sew a seam down each long side, sewing 1½in/3.5cm from the edge of your fabric **[C]**.

8. Turn the two long borders back so that the right sides are facing up and press the seams flat. Lay your shorter, end border pieces on top of the table runner, with right sides facing and pin. Sew a seam, again, 1½in/3.5cm from the edge of your fabric **[D]**. Turn back the end border pieces and press the seam flat.

9. Press the edge of one long border strip under by ¾in/2cm, then fold the strip in half so the edge lies just inside the stitch line and press again. Repeat for the other long strip, then for the two short end strips.

10. Slip stitch [see page 9] the folded edge in place to the backing fabric, folding the corners over as shown **[E]**.

C. Sewing the long border strips in place.

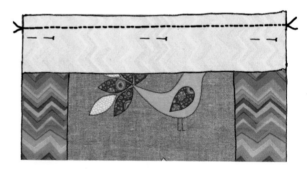

D. Adding the short border strips.

E. Slip stitching the folded border edge.

THE PLACEMAT ALTERNATIVE

I turned the design for the runner into little placemats, with just one bird per mat. You can have them all facing the same direction or switch the directions, like the runner. The edging for the mat is made in the same way as the runner, but is just ⅝in/1.5cm wide and each mat measures 10 x 13½in/26 x 34cm. The fabrics used for this mat are the same as those for the runner, but you could use different colorways for each mat.

BETH'S TIP
If you want to protect your table from scorch marks from hot plates, then sandwich a layer of batting between the top and backing fabrics, before applying the contrasting border.

STYLIZED TREE CUSHION

I made this retro version of the tree pillow on a striking red background fabric and turned the tree motif into a more stylized, simplified version. Using solid fabric for the "trunk and branches" and patterned fabric for the "leaves," gives it a very different look. Why not try your own design versions, too? I adapted the tree further for the tote bag on page 46.

THINGS YOU NEED

✤ Tree template on page 128
✤ Red cotton fabric, approx ½yd/½m
✤ Large sheet of ⅛in/1mm thick yellow felt
✤ Large sheet of ⅛in/1mm thick beige felt
✤ Circles or spots patterned cotton fabric, for your tree decorations or scraps of leftover fabric
✤ Fusible web
✤ Embroidery floss in coordinating colors and embroidery needle
✤ Basic sewing kit
✤ Sewing machine and matching thread
✤ Pillow form (cushion pad), 9½ x 19¾in/24 x 50cm

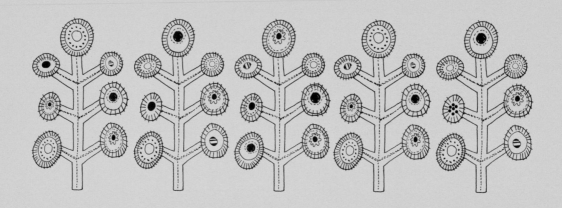

MAKING THE CUSHION

FINISHED SIZE
9½ x 19¾in/24 x 50cm

CUTTING OUT
FROM RED COTTON
Cut 1: 10¼ x 20¾in/26 x 53cm rectangle
Cut 2: 10¼ x 11½in/26 x 29cm rectangles
FROM YELLOW FELT
Cut 2: 5½ x 3¼in/14 x 8cm rectangles
FROM BEIGE FELT
Cut 3: 5½ x 3¼in/14 x 8cm rectangles
FROM PATTERNED COTTONS
Enough for 35 circles, 1in/2.5cm diameter
NOTE: All measurements include ⅜in/1cm
    seam allowance unless otherwise stated.

> **BETH'S TIP**
> Try cutting larger
> circles of patterned
> fabric for the "tops" of
> your trees and slightly
> smaller circles for the
> lower branches—this will
> make your tree look well
> proportioned and a little
> more interesting than
> having all the circles
> the same size.

ATTACHING THE TREES

1. Copy the tree template on page 128 and pin it to the piece of felt. Cut out five tree motifs: three beige, two yellow **(A)**.

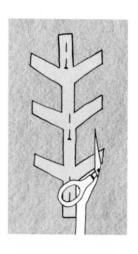

A. Cutting out the templates from felt.

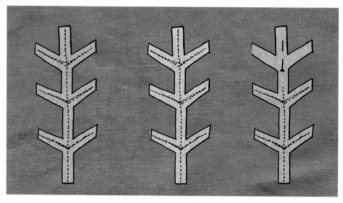

B. Positioning the felt trees on the fabric.

2. Pin the felt tree to the rectangle of fabric, about 4in/10cm apart and 2¼in/5.5cm up from the bottom edge, alternating the color of the trees. Use running stitch on your sewing machine (or backstitch by hand, see page 9) to sew the trees in place along the center of the trunk and branches **(B)**.

ATTACHING THE CIRCLES

3. Iron a piece of fusible web onto the wrong side of the patterned fabric for the circles.

4. Cut out circles of fabric following the pattern **(C)**; you'll need seven circles per tree (35 in total).

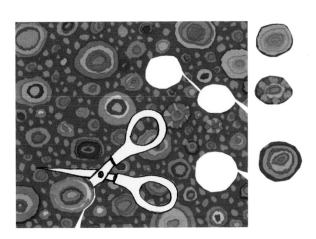

C. Cutting out 35 circles from spotty fabric.

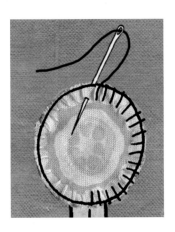

D. Appliqué stitching the fabric circles in place.

FINISHING THE CUSHION

7. Follow the instructions on page 15 for finishing your cushion back. Insert the pillow form and your cushion is complete!

5. Peel off the backing. Position the circles, one at the end of each branch, and iron in place.

6. Using a coordinating color of embroidery floss, appliqué stitch (see page 10) around the edge of the circles to secure and embellish **(D)**.

FISH ON A LINE

These jolly fish not only look good, but
smell great too—they are filled with
lavender so you can hang them in the
bathroom or your bedroom. Alternatively,
you could stuff them with batting if you
just want to use them as a decorative
hanging or even add a little catnip to
make a toy for your favorite feline
friend. Each step of this project can
either be sewn on a machine, or by hand.

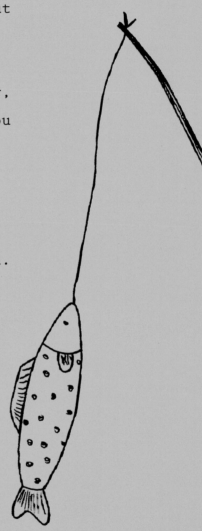

THINGS YOU NEED

- Fish template on page 131
- Solid-color cotton fabric
- Spotty bright cotton fabric
- Scraps of felt in contrasting colors
- Embroidery floss in contrasting colors
  and embroidery needle
- Thick twine or colored yarn
- Basic sewing kit
- Dried lavender

MAKING THE FISH

FINISHED SIZE
3¼ x 8¼in/8 x 21cm

CUTTING OUT (PER FISH)
FROM SOLID-COLOR COTTON
Cut 2: 2¾ x 2¾in/7 x 7cm squares
FROM SPOTTY BRIGHT COTTON
Cut 2: 4 x 6in/10 x 15cm rectangles
FROM FELT
Cut 1: 5 x 4in/13 x 10cm rectangle

PREPARING THE PIECES

1. Copy the templates on page 131. Place the spotty fabric pieces wrong sides together and pin the templates to both pieces. Cut out to make two body pieces, cutting approx ¼in/5mm outside the line for a seam allowance. Do the same with the solid-color cotton fabric to cut out two head pieces.

2. From felt, cut two tail pieces, two side fin pieces, and two top fin pieces.

3. Stitch the two tail pieces together, using a contrasting embroidery floss and lines of continuous running stitch. Start by sewing a line of running stitch, then go back and sew along the same line of stitching, filling in the "gaps" with your next stitches, as shown. Repeat to stitch five lines **(A)**.

4. Sew the two top fins together in the same way as the tail and add lines of continuous running stitch. Add three lines of continuous running stitch to each of the side fins **(B)**.

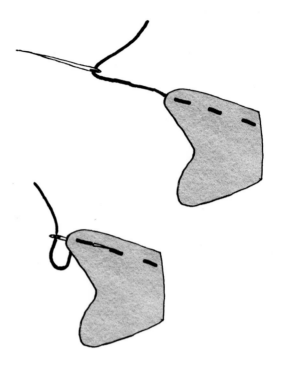

A. Sewing lines of continuous running stitch on the tail.

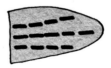

B. Adding lines of continuous running stitch on the top and side fins.

MAKING THE FISH

5. Sew one side fin to each body piece, onto the right side of your fabric. Position your fin about ¾in/2cm up from the bottom edge **(C)**.

6. Pin a head to a body piece, right sides together, and machine- or hand-sew in place (over the fin). Repeat for the other body piece **(D)**. Open out and press the head flat.

7. Sew the tail and top fin onto the right side of one of the body pieces, as shown **(E)**.

8. Take a length of twine or yarn and secure the "fishing line" with a couple of stitches at the tip of the head. Make sure that the line is positioned along the body **(F)**.

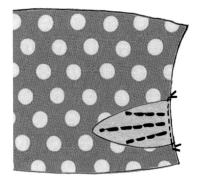

C. Sewing the side fin to the body.

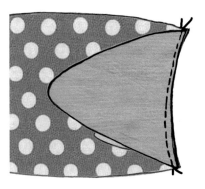

D. Sewing the head piece in place.

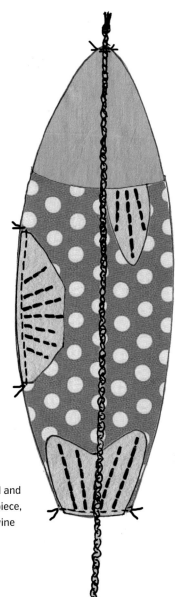

E & F. Sewing the tail and top fin to one body piece, and attaching the twine to the head.

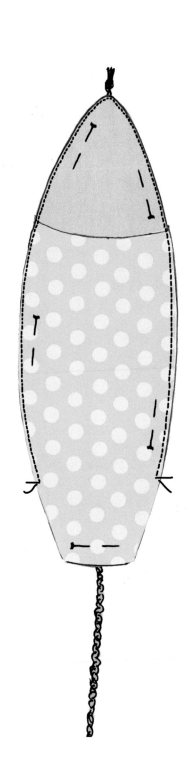

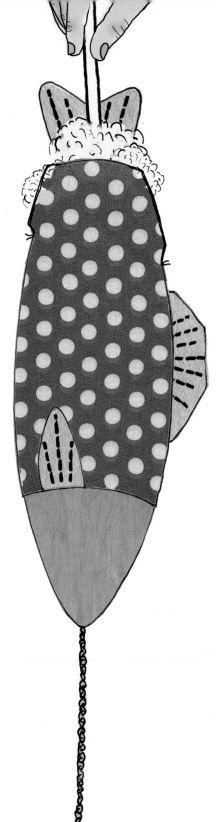

9. Pin the second body piece on top, right sides together, and machine- or hand-sew the seam close to the edge, stopping short to leave the tail end open, as shown **(G)**. Turn right side out through the end and press flat.

STUFFING THE FISH

10. You can either fill your fish with stuffing, or lavender, or catnip. Using a pencil or the blunt end of a knitting needle, push the stuffing down into the head of your fish, then stuff the whole of the fish, leaving it nice and rounded **(H)**.

11. Now pin the tail end of the fish together, folding under the raw edges, and slip stitch (see page 9) both sides together **(I)**.

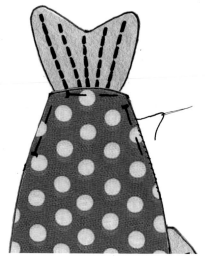

G. Sewing the body pieces, right sides together.

H. Stuffing the fish.

I. Slip stitching the end closed.

STUFFED FISH ALTERNATIVE

Instead of hanging your fish, increase the size of the templates to make a larger version as a stuffed toy for a child. With bright prints and toy stuffing, the simple fish will be the perfect shape for little hands to grasp. It might be fun to make a "family" of fish in three different sizes. You could also make a little version, filled with catnip, as a cat toy.

BETH'S TIP
Stuffing the fish can be a little tricky. To prevent stuffing from falling out, hold your fish vertically, head down and tail side uppermost. Use a pencil to push the batting down into the head of the fish.

HANGING ELEPHANTS

This sweet hanging would be lovely in a child's nursery or in a playroom. It is really easy to make—there are no seams and felt is great to sew with, as it doesn't fray at all! All the elephants are made the same way, it is just the felt colors that vary. If you'd rather make your elephants from patterned fabric, iron interfacing onto the wrong side of your fabric before you cut out the shapes, to reduce fraying.

THINGS YOU NEED

* Elephant templates on page 131
* Wool felt in two colors
* Scraps of patterned fabric (two colorways of the same print)
* Tapestry yarn or knitting yarn, for tails and to hang your elephants
* Beads
* Basic sewing kit
* Embroidery floss and embroidery needle
* White (PVA) or fabric glue
* Toy stuffing or fiberfill

MAKING THE ELEPHANTS

FINISHED SIZE
One elephant: 3 x 3½in/8 x 9cm

CUTTING OUT (PER ELEPHANT)
FROM FELT (FOR BODY)
Cut 2: 4 x 6in/10 x 15cm rectangles
FROM PATTERNED FABRIC (FOR EARS)
Cut 4: 2 x 2in/5 x 5cm squares

PREPARATION
1. Copy the templates on page 131. Layer two pieces of matching felt together, pin the body template to one side and cut out **(A)**.

2. For the ears, lay two pieces of patterned fabric wrong sides together and pin your template in place. Cut out and repeat for the second ear with the remaining two pieces of fabric **(B)**.

SEWING THE ELEPHANT
3. Pin the two ear pieces wrong sides together. Using embroidery floss, blanket stitch (see page 11) the two pieces together **(C)**. Once you get back to where you started, don't tie off your thread but leave a length free to sew the ear onto the body. Repeat for the other ear.

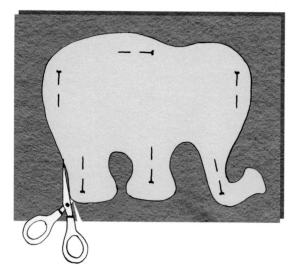

A. Cutting the body shape from two layers of felt.

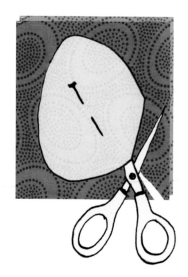

B. Cutting the ears from two pieces of fabric.

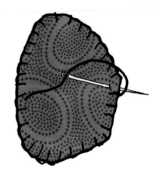

C. Blanket stitching the ear pieces together.

SEWING UP THE ELEPHANT

4. Using the free length of thread, sew the ear to the body of your elephant about 1in/2.5cm in from the head, using five or six stitches along the straight edge of the ear. Repeat for the other side of the elephant's body **(D)**.

5. To sew the eye, make a large cross stitch (see page 10) using embroidery floss, as shown **(E)**. Repeat for the other body piece.

6. To create the tail, cut a short length of embroidery floss, about 2¾in/7cm long, and tie a knot in one end. Dab a little glue on the other end and press in place on the wrong side of one of the body pieces **(F)**.

7. Pin the two body pieces wrong sides together, encasing the tail in between. Using blanket stitch, sew the body together, leaving an opening of about 1½in/4cm along the back to insert the stuffing. Keep your needle and thread attached.

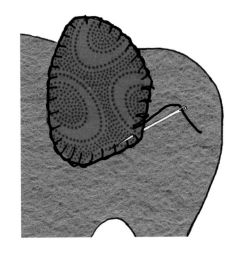

D. Sewing the ear to the head.

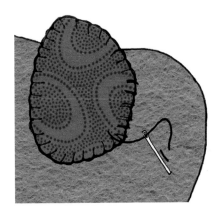

E. Adding the eye with a large cross stitch.

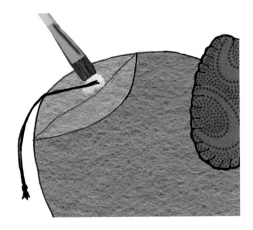

F. Gluing the tail in place.

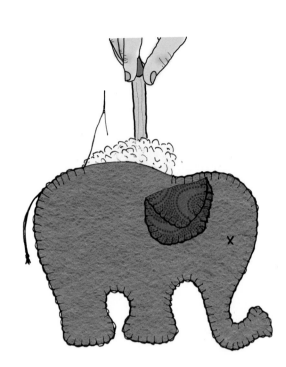

G. Stuffing the elephant with filling.

H. Threading on the elephants.

STUFFING THE ELEPHANT

8. Stuff the body with small tufts of stuffing, using a pencil or knitting needle to push small amounts of filling down into the legs and trunk **(G)**. Picking up the thread, continue using blanket stitch to sew up the gap, enclosing the stuffing.

9. Repeat steps 1–8 twice, to make a total of three stuffed elephants.

STRINGING THE ELEPHANTS

10. Thread a length of tapestry yarn about 1yd/1m long through a long needle and tie several knots in the end. Following the instructions on page 15, thread several glass or ceramic beads to weight your hanging.

11. Pull the needle through the center of the first elephant between its legs and out through the middle of its back. Check that the elephant hangs straight and alter the position of the thread if not **(H)**. Pass the thread through the second and the third elephant, adjusting as you go. Finish off by tying a loop for hanging.

SARDINE PANEL

Customize this idea to make a panel to match the size of your bathroom or restroom window. You can add a row of sardine-style fish to an existing solid-color blind, or make your own in just a few steps. When calculating the amount of fabric required, you need to measure your window. Measure the width of the window and decide whether your panel will hang across the architrave or inside the recess and measure this distance. Now measure the height from the top of the window recess or architrave to the sill, this is the drop. Your fabric panel can hang above the sill, if you prefer.

THINGS YOU NEED

* Sardine template on page 129
* Solid-color cotton, linen, or similar fabric (or an existing blind)
* ¼yd/¼m patterned fabric, for sardines
* 1yd/1m coordinating fabric, for border
* Fusible web
* Basic sewing kit
* Five small buttons, for eyes
* Embroidery floss in a contrasting color and embroidery needle
* Sewing machine and matching thread

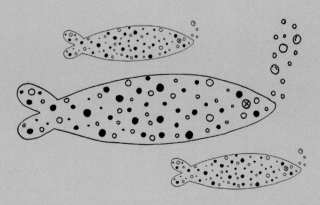

MAKING THE PANEL

FINISHED SIZE

To fit your window—see page 77

CUTTING OUT

FROM SOLID-COLOR COTTON OR LINEN
See page 77 for calculating fabric quantity
FROM PATTERNED FABRIC (FOR SARDINES)
8¾ x 2½in/22 x 6cm for each sardine
FROM PATTERNED FABRIC (FOR BORDER)
Cut 2: 34¾ x 7in/88 x 18cm rectangles
Cut 2: 23 x 7in/58 x 18cm rectangles

APPLYING THE SARDINES

1. Copy the sardine template on page 129. Iron fusible web to the wrong side of the patterned fabric rectangle for your sardines and draw around the sardine template. Cut out and repeat to make five sardines in total (or the number required for your blind width).

2. Peel off the fusible web backing and lay your sardines in place on the blind fabric. Position them about 4in/10cm from the bottom edge of the fabric and alternate them so that they are lying top to tail. Iron in place.

3. Using embroidery floss in a contrasting color, appliqué stitch (see page 10) around the outline of each fish **(A)**. Then give each of your fish an eye by sewing a button in place.

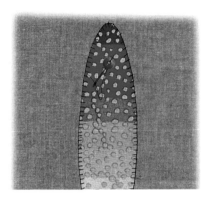

A. Embellishing the sardines with appliqué stitching.

ADDING THE BORDER

4. Position one long border piece along one long edge, with right sides facing, leaving a ⅝in/1.5cm overlap at the bottom corner. Sew the seam, taking a ⅜in/1cm seam allowance. Iron flat and repeat on the opposite edge and the two short edges **(B)**.

B. Adding the side and bottom borders.

5. Press under a ¼in/5mm turning along the raw edge of the border strip. Then press the border strip in half to the wrong side of the blind. Pin so that the edge lies just inside the stitch line. Slip stitch down the fold (see page 9), taking care not to let the stitches show on the right side of your fabric **(C)**. Work along one edge of your blind at a time.

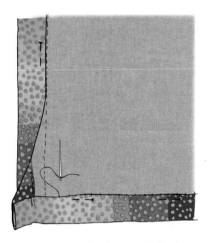

C. Slip stitching the border in place on the back.

BETH'S TIP
You can hang your window panel in a number of ways: simply fold over the top border and stitch a channel for threading through a pole or hanging wire, or attach the top of the panel to a wire or rod with drapery clips for an instant solution. If you want more privacy, use the central fabric double, and remember to double the fabric quantity.

HOUSE DOORSTOP

This is a great, easy but very effective project that transforms a plain store-bought doorstop into a decorative object—you'll want to have one in every room! This design has a house appliquéd to each side of the doorstop, repeating two colorways. You could swap the house motif for one of the other motifs in the book—the owl on page 84 or the elephant on page 70, would look fantastic, too.

THINGS YOU NEED

- Store-bought square doorstop, approx 7 x 7 x 7in/18 x 18 x 18cm
- House templates on page 128
- Seam ripper or small scissors
- Felt in three different colors
- Embroidery floss in contrasting colors and embroidery needle
- Fading fabric marker or water-soluble pen
- Basic sewing kit

MAKING THE HOUSE DOORSTOP

FINISHED SIZE
7 x 7 x 7in/18 x 18 x 18cm

PREPARATION

1. Take your doorstop and unpick three seams from the bottom edge. Remove the stuffing and any weights and set aside.

2. Copy the templates on page 128 and draw around the house and roof shapes on the pieces of felt to make four houses and four roofs. Put the paper door template aside.

SEWING THE HOUSE

3. Pin one house to one side of the doorstop, about 1in/2.5cm from the bottom edge. Using backstitch (see page 9), sew around the windows just in from the edge **(A)**. Using running stitch (see page 10), sew just inside the outline of the house.

4. Pin the roof in place so it fits just on top of the house. Using running stitch, sew the roof just in from the edge **(B)**.

5. Taking a different color embroidery floss (I used all 6 strands for a thick line), sew a long cross in each window to create the window panes **(C)**.

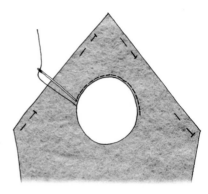

A. Backstitching around the window.

B. Pinning the roof in place.

> **BETH'S TIP**
> To cut out your windows, fold the felt in half through the window, make a cross incision in the center of the window shape, then unfold. Insert your scissors into the incision and cut around the inside of the shape.

C. Sewing the window panes with a large cross.

6. Position the door template on the felt house and draw around it using a fading fabric marker or water-soluble pen.

7. Using satin stitch (see page 10), start at the bottom of the door and sew one long stitch all the way across, following the lines you have just drawn. Continue until you have filled in the door shape **(D)**. For the door handle, sew a French knot (see page 11) on the right-hand side of the door.

8. Repeat steps 3–8 on the other three sides of the doorstop until you have four houses, one on each side.

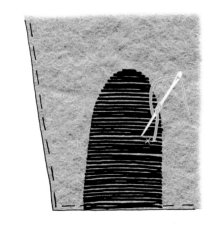

D. Satin stitching the door.

FINISHING THE DOORSTOP

9. Turn the doorstop upside down and put the stuffing and weight back inside. Pin the seams together and slip stitch (see page 9) the sides closed.

ALTERNATIVE CARD PROJECT

Sew the house onto a rectangle of card or fabric and attach this to a greeting card blank with the words "new home" sewn above, to make a sweet house warming card.

BEADY OWL CARD

Everybody loves receiving a card, especially one that has been handmade. You can tailor this card for any occasion by adding a written or embroidered greeting. An alternative use for the owl is shown on page 87.

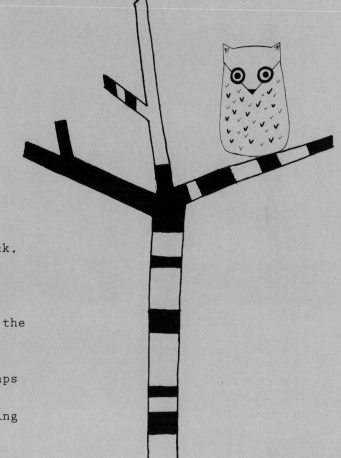

THINGS YOU NEED

* Owl templates on page 130
* Card blank or piece of cardstock, approx 6 x 8in/15 x 21cm
* Iron-on interfacing
* Fusible web
* Solid-color cotton fabric, for the background, 4¼ x 3¼in/11 x 8cm
* Patterned cotton fabric in two patterns for the owl, plus scraps of fabric for the eyes
* Embroidery floss or cotton sewing thread and needle
* Fabric glue
* Basic sewing kit

MAKING THE BEADY OWL CARD

FINISHED SIZE
Approx 6 x 4in/15 x 10cm

PREPARATION
1. Iron a piece of interfacing onto the wrong side of your solid-color cotton and trim to 4 x 3in/10 x 7.5cm. Iron fusible web to the wrong side of the fabric for the owl.

2. Copy the templates and transfer them to the paper backing. Cut out the head and body pieces. Cut out two circles about ½in/12mm and ¾in/2cm diameter, for each eye.

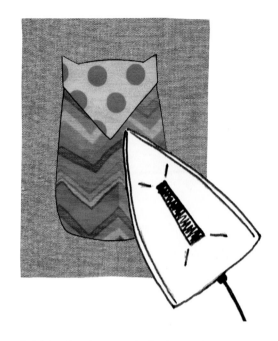
A. Ironing the shapes to the background.

ATTACHING THE OWL
3. Peel the paper backing from the owl's body and iron in place in the middle of the solid fabric rectangle, then iron the owl's head on top of the body **(A)**.

4. Using one strand of embroidery floss or sewing thread, blanket stitch (see page 11) around all the raw edges **(B)**.

5. Iron the eyes in place, layering the smaller eye on the larger one. Sew a large cross stitch (see page 10) in each eye **(C)**.

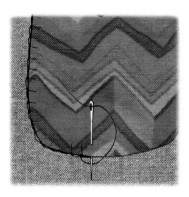
B. Blanket stitching the edge.

C. Adding a cross stitch to the eyes.

MAKING THE CARD

6. Fold the card in half if you don't have a card blank. Using a very small amount of fabric glue, stick the appliquéd piece of cotton centered on the front of the card.

7. Use a needle to make holes through the card where you are going to sew blanket stitch, about ⅜in/1cm apart and ⅜in/1cm deep **(D)**.

8. Using embroidery floss, blanket stitch around the cotton rectangle to secure the fabric to the card, using your pre-punched holes **(E)**.

D. Needle-punching holes in the card.

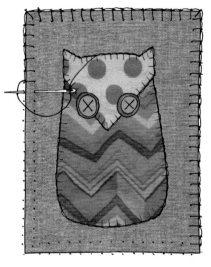

E. Blanket stitching to the card through the pre-punched holes.

ALTERNATIVE BAG PROJECT

This little owl is so versatile, you could add him to a purse, a bag, or a cushion. Try increasing the size of the owl template to fit a shopping bag. Apply fusible web onto the back of your fabric piece, cut out, and sew in place on a plain tote bag using blanket stitch (see page 11).

CIRCLES CUSHION

This is a fantastic use of leftover fabrics from other projects, and is a bold, bright statement. I have made this cushion with an enclosed cover, which means it cannot be removed. Alternatively, you can make the cover with an envelope back, following the instructions on page 14.

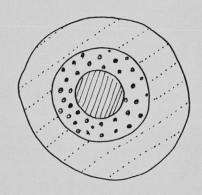

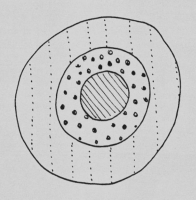

THINGS YOU NEED

* Bright colored cotton in three different patterns
* Solid-color cotton, for background
* Circle templates, see tip
* Fusible web
* Embroidery floss in contrasting colors and embroidery needle
* Basic sewing kit
* Sewing machine and matching thread
* 16 x 16in/40 x 40cm pillow form (cushion pad)

MAKING THE CIRCLES CUSHION

FINISHED SIZE
16 x 16in/40 x 40cm

CUTTING OUT
FROM BRIGHT PATTERNED COTTON
For each large circle, cut 1: 14in/36cm square
For each medium circle, cut 1: 10½in/27cm square
For each small circle, cut 1: 7in/18cm square
FROM SOLID-COLOR COTTON
Cut 2: 16½in/42cm squares
NOTE: All measurements include ⅝in/1.5cm seam
   allowance unless otherwise stated.

BETH'S TIP
To create the circle templates,
make paper templates either
using a compass or just find
3 different circular things
around the house and draw around
them onto the fusible web paper
backing, then cut out. You can
vary the diameters to suit what
you have to hand, ensuring you
have a large, medium, and small.

PREPARATION
1. Apply fusible web to the wrong side of all pieces of
patterned fabric. Make paper templates of circles
with a diameter of 4in/10cm, 3in/7.5cm, 1½in/4cm
(see tip, below), then draw around them on the
paper backing to make 9 large (A), 9 medium (B),
and 9 small circles (C). Cut out.

APPLYING THE CIRCLES
2. Position the circles (first A, then B, then C) onto
the right side of one piece of background fabric.
Lay them out evenly, leaving a 2½in/6cm border
around the edges of the background fabric. Once
you are happy with the positioning, remove the
paper backing and iron in place **(A)**.

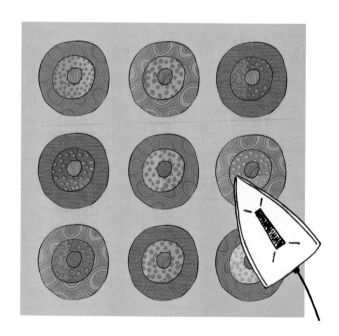

A. Ironing the circles in place.

3. Using one strand of embroidery floss in a contrasting color, sew around each circle at a time, using long appliqué stitches (see page 10) **(B)**. Alternatively, you could use zig-zag stitch on your sewing machine.

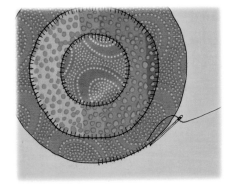

B. Stitching the circles to the cushion front.

ASSEMBLING THE CUSHION

4. On a flat surface, lay out one piece of solid cotton right side up with the appliquéd piece of cotton right side down. Pin the pieces together.

5. Machine sew around three edges of the cover, taking a ⅝in/1.5cm seam, leaving one edge open.

6. Trim the raw edges and clip the corners. Turn the cover right side out and press. Stuff with a 16 x 16in/40 x 40cm pillow form.

7. Turn under and pin the open edge, then slip stitch (see page 9) the edge closed using matching thread.

EMBROIDERED SLIPPERS

No one will mistake these slippers as not being yours once you've embroidered them with your initial! Using pre-cut insoles makes shaping the slipper easy, and a few decorative stitches give the design a folksy, homey feel. Felt can be slippery, so if you live in a house with all wooden floors you could substitute the bottom felt sole with a non-slip fabric.

THINGS YOU NEED

- Slipper and Letter templates on pages 131 and 132
- A pair of store-bought insoles in your shoe size
- Large sheet of ⅛in/3mm thick felt, at least 16in/40cm square
- Fading fabric marker or water-soluble pen
- Tapestry yarn and thin yarn needle
- Embroidery floss and embroidery needle
- Rubber thimble (optional)
- Basic sewing kit
- Fabric glue

MAKING THE EMBROIDERED SLIPPERS

FINISHED SIZE
To fit your shoe size

PREPARATION

1. Copy the template on page 131 and cut out the slipper uppers pattern pieces. Copy your chosen letter and cut it out from paper, following the tip on page 22 for tricky letters.

2. Trim your insoles to a couple of sizes larger all round than your normal shoe size, making them quite square shaped at the toes. Draw around the trimmed insoles onto the felt, adding about ⅜in/1cm around all sides. Cut out two felt shapes for the right foot and two for the left.

ADDING THE STITCHES

3. Following the stitch guide on pages 131, embroider the slipper uppers. Start with blanket stitch (see page 11) down the straight edge. Add the French knots and running stitch (see pages 11 and 10) detail next **(A)**.

4. With a fading fabric marker or water-soluble pen, mark a dot where you are going to sew each of your star stitches, leaving an empty space in the middle for your letter. Sew the stars with vertical and horizontal cross stitches, then stitch diagonal cross stitches (see page 10) over the top **(B)**.

5. Pin the paper letter template to the slipper upper in the space. Draw around the template with a fabric marker or water-soluble pen **(C)**. Using satin stitch (see page 10), embroider the letter. To neaten your letter, sew a line of backstitch around the outline.

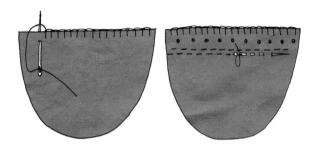

A. Embroidering the slipper uppers.

B. Marking and sewing the star stitches.

C. Marking the letter template.

FINISHING THE SLIPPERS

6. Brush a small amount of fabric glue on both sides of your insole, then stick two matching felt feet pieces to the top and bottom so you have a felt, insole, felt "sandwich" **(D)**.

7. Pin the slipper upper to the felt sole. Using 6 strands of embroidery floss, blanket stitch all the way around your slipper, through all the layers **(E)**. Repeat steps 2–7 to make the second slipper.

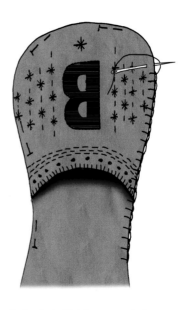

D. Making the felt "sandwich" for the sole.

E. Blanket stitching around all the edges.

BETH'S TIP
For embroidering the slippers, either use tapestry yarn or embroidery floss. Embroidery floss is easier to pull through the felt than yarn, as it is thinner. If using tapestry yarn, I suggest using a rubber thimble to protect your fingers. If you want to do less embroidery, cut the letter from a contrasting colored felt instead, and stitch to the slipper upper using running stitches.

FLOWER GARLAND

This is a beautiful, simple project that involves very little sewing and would look fabulous draped over a door, mirror, or picture frame, or tacked to a mantelpiece. You can use coordinating fabrics, or it's perfect for using up scraps of leftover fabric from other projects. The flower motif is infinitely adaptable—attach it to bags or cushions, or transform it into a brooch to liven up a jacket or accessorize your purse.

THINGS YOU NEED

- Flower garland templates on page 128
- Patterned fabric in coordinating colors
- Scraps of felt
- Fusible web
- Embroidery floss and embroidery needle
- Basic sewing kit
- Chunky yarn in a contrasting color

MAKING THE FLOWER GARLAND

FINISHED SIZE
Length: 3yd/3m

CUTTING OUT
FROM PATTERNED FABRIC
Cut 32: 5½in/14cm squares
FROM SCRAPS OF FELT
Cut 8: ½in x ⅜in/ 1.3 x 1cm rectangles

PREPARATION
1. Iron fusible web to the wrong side of 16 squares of fabric. Peel off the backing and iron the other 16 squares on top, to give you 16 double-sided pairs.

2. Copy the flower garland templates on page 128. Pin them to your double-sided fabric square and cut out four of each template.

BETH'S TIP
There is no set rule for how to combine fabrics and patterns. I simply arranged them so that no two of the same fabrics were on each side of each flower, and no two of the same fabrics showed on each finished double flower. You can end up with many different combinations, or if you prefer, choose two fabrics and make all your flowers from these two fabrics, alternating which fabric you use for which flower shape.

MAKING THE FLOWERS
3. For each flower, fold in half, then in quarters, and score along the fold lines with your fingernails, this will give the flowers some shape **(A)**. Unfold. Pair up the large flower with the smaller flower centers.

4. Take your first small flower center and pinch it together from the back. Sew a few stitches approximately ⅜in/1cm from the pinching point. Keep the needle and thread attached **(B)**. Open the flower flat and check the 3-D effect; pinch again and sew a few more stitches if the shape isn't pronounced enough.

5. Using the same thread (still attached to your small flower) insert the needle through the middle of the large flower and sew a few stitches in the back to secure the center in place **(C)**.

6. Pinch the flowers together and sew a few stitches to create the 3-D effect, as in step 4. Secure the thread and open out the flowers.

7. Now take a small felt rectangle and sew it to the center of your flower with three or four long stitches on top of each other **(D)**. Take the needle to the back, knot the thread, and leave a long tail to attach the flower to the knitted yarn. Repeat steps 4–7 to make the remaining two flowers.

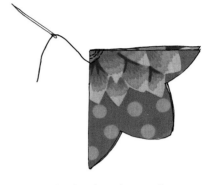

A. Folding each flower shape in half, then in quarters.

B. Sewing the point together.

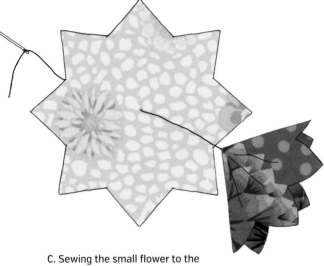

C. Sewing the small flower to the larger flower.

D. Sewing a felt rectangle to the flower center.

MAKING THE FINGER KNITTED LENGTH

8. Make a slip knot in the end of the yarn, still attached to the ball, and slip it onto your writing hand thumb **(E)**. Hold the long tail in your opposite hand and wind it around your thumb, from inside to outside **(F)**.

9. Now slip the first loop over the length you just looped around your thumb and off your thumb **(G)**. You will now have one loop on your thumb and a loose loop under your thumb **(H)**. Tighten by pulling on the two lengths of yarn one at a time (not too tight). Wind the tail around your thumb again and repeat; you will create a chain of loops, making a knitted length **(I)**.

10. Using the long tail of thread on each flower, sew them to the knitted length of yarn, about 12in/30cm apart.

> **BETH'S TIP**
> The four pattern pieces create two different flower combinations; a large curved petal flower with a triangle petal flower middle, and a large straight edge triangle flower with a smaller curved petal flower middle.

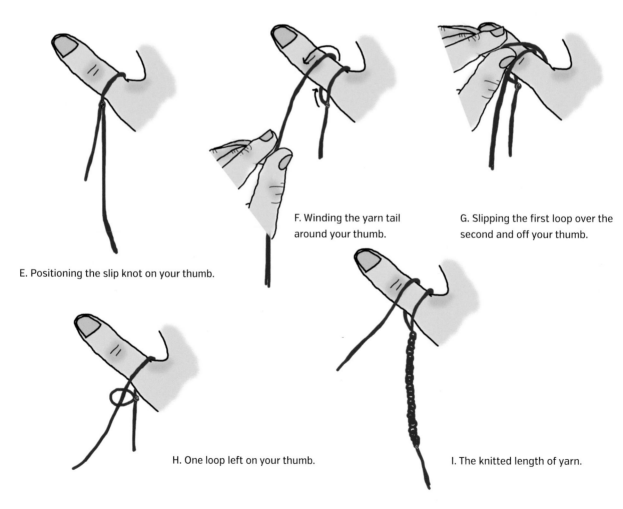

E. Positioning the slip knot on your thumb.

F. Winding the yarn tail around your thumb.

G. Slipping the first loop over the second and off your thumb.

H. One loop left on your thumb.

I. The knitted length of yarn.

FLOWER GARLAND

BIRD TOTE BAG

This is a fantastic, quick-and-easy project that will transform a plain tote or shopping bag into a bright and fun bag you'll want to use everyday. It's a great excuse to use pretty patterned fabrics; I chose just two contrasting colors, but you could use a different pattern or colorway for each rectangle, if you like.

THINGS YOU NEED

* Bird template on page 131
* Existing bright solid-color tote or shopping bag
* Patterned fabric, in two coordinating colors or designs
* Solid-color bright cotton fabric in four different colors
* Fusible web
* Embroidery floss and embroidery needle
* Basic sewing kit

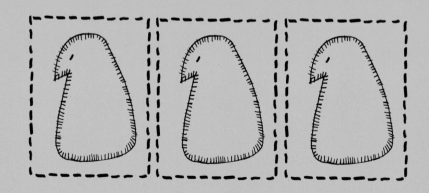

MAKING THE BIRD TOTE BAG

FINISHED SIZE
Same size as your bag

CUTTING OUT
FROM PATTERNED FABRIC
Cut 4: 4¼ x 3¼in/10.5 x 8cm rectangles
FROM SOLID-COLOR BRIGHT FABRIC
Cut 4: 2½ x 3½in/6 x 9cm rectangles
FROM FUSIBLE WEB
Cut 4: 4¼ x 3¼in/10.5 x 8cm rectangles
Cut 4: 2½ x 3½in/6 x 9cm rectangles

PREPARATION
1. Iron the large pieces of fusible web to the wrong side of the large fabric rectangles. Iron the smaller rectangles of web onto the wrong side of the pieces of bright cotton.

2. Copy the bird template on page 131. Draw around the bird motif (remember to flip the template) onto the fusbile web backing paper on the bright rectangles and cut out.

ATTACHING THE FABRIC
3. Peel off the paper backing from one large fabric rectangle and position on the tote bag, about 2½in/6cm from the bottom of the bag and ⅝in/1.5cm from the sides. Press in place with an iron. Repeat to add the remaining rectangles, equally spaced across the bag [A].

4. Peel off the backing paper and position your birds in the middle of each printed rectangle on your bag. Iron in place [B].

A. Positioning the rectangles on the bag.

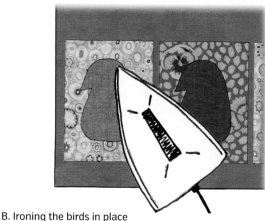

B. Ironing the birds in place on the fabric rectangles.

> BETH'S TIP
> When you are sewing the blanket stitch detail around the rectangles and birds, be careful not to sew both sides of the bag together. Grab the fabric of the bag in your non-sewing hand from the top, it will gather and crease but you can iron these creases out once you've finished the project.

5. Using embroidery floss, blanket stitch (see page 11) around the rectangles of fabric, then sew around each bird in a contrasting color.

ALTERNATIVE NEEDLECASE PROJECT

Use just one bird to make a sweet needlecase to give to a friend.

Follow steps 1 and 2 and attach to the right-hand end of a 5 x 8in/13 x 20cm rectangle of thick felt, using blanket stitch (see page 11). Blanket stitch all the way around the edge of the felt rectangle. Fold the rectangle in half, to make a book. Cut a slightly smaller rectangle from felt, fold it in half and insert it into the larger rectangle, to make the "pages." Thread a length of ribbon through all layers of felt and tie a bow on the outside to finish your needlecase "book."

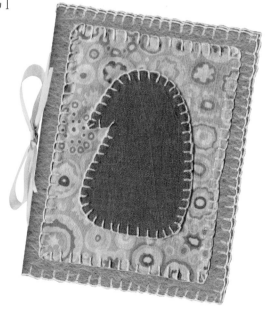

KIT AND KAT STUFFED CATS

These fabric cats are a great project to either make as a gift or just to adorn your mantelpiece or windowsill. I have made two cats and embroidered their names "Kit" and "Kat" on their collars. How about creating a whole family of cats by reducing the template and making a few kittens, too!

THINGS YOU NEED

* Cat templates on page 130
* ¼yd/¼m patterned fabric, per cat
* Felt
* Iron-on interfacing
* Embroidery floss in a contrasting color and embroidery needle
* Basic sewing kit
* Batting (wadding)
* Beads

MAKING THE STUFFED CATS

FINISHED SIZE
Approx 10 x 5in/25 x 12cm

CUTTING OUT
FROM PATTERNED FABRIC
Cut 2: 12 x 6¼in/30 x 16cm rectangles
FROM IRON-ON INTERFACING
Cut 2: 12 x 6¼in/30 x 16cm rectangles
FROM FELT
Cut 1: 8¾ x 6in/22 x 15cm rectangle, for base

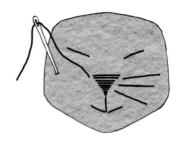

A. Embroidering the face details.

PREPARATION
1. Copy the templates on page 130 and cut out the face and tummy pieces from felt. Iron interfacing onto the wrong side of the pieces of patterned fabric, then cut out the front and back body pieces.

STITCHING THE CAT
2. Using embroidery floss in a contrasting color, embroider your cat's face following the stitch guide on the template. Use satin stitch for the nose and long straight stitches for the eyes and whiskers **(A)**.

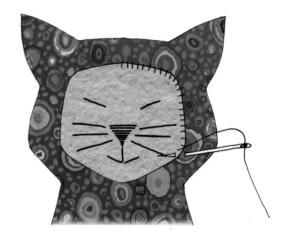

B. Stitching the face with appliqué stitches.

3. Pin the embroidered face to the right side of a body piece. Using either one strand of embroidery floss in a similar color or sewing thread, stitch the face in place with small appliqué stitches across the edge (see page 10) **(B)**. Repeat to attach the tummy.

4. Pin the front and back body pieces wrong sides together. Using blanket stitch (see page 11), sew all the way around the cat, sewing the back and front cat pieces together and making sure to leave the bottom edge unstitched **(C)**.

C. Blanket stitching the front and back together.

FINISHING THE CAT

5. Take two small pieces of stuffing and carefully push them down into your cat's ears using a pencil or the blunt end of a knitting needle. Next, take a continuous piece of wadding and stuff your cat, pushing the wadding a little at a time down into your cat, making sure you stuff the head well.

6. Once stuffed, pin the base felt piece to the stuffed cat, to give a base to stand on. Using blanket stitch, sew all the way around the base, sewing the piece of felt to the front and back **(D)**.

7. To make a collar, cut a 4-in/10-cm length of felt about ⅜in/1cm wide. Using backstitch (see page 9), sew your cat's name to the collar **(E)** and add a bead for a bell. Then wrap the collar around your cat's neck, and sew a few overstitches where the two ends meet to secure.

E. Backstitching the name to the felt collar.

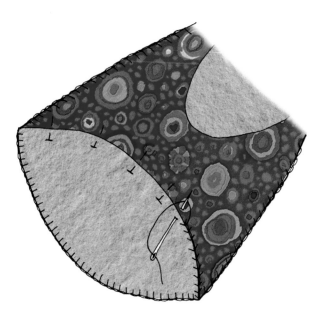

D. Blanket stitching the base in place.

BETH'S TIP
When pinning and sewing the felt base piece, turn the cat upside down—this will prevent any stuffing from escaping and will be much easier when sewing the felt and fabric together with blanket stitch. For added decoration, you could stitch three small buttons down the center of the front felt panel.

THE OWL AND THE PUSSYCAT WALL TIDY

Hide away all your sewing or crafty bits and bobs in this cute wall tidy. You can change the length and size of the pockets to suit the items you want to tidy away and add more motifs if you like.

THINGS YOU NEED

* Owl and cat templates on page 130
* ½yd/½m patterned fabric, for pockets
* 24in/60cm solid-color cotton fabric, for pockets
* 24in/60m felt or woolen fabric, for backing
* Bias binding
* Fusible web
* Embroidery floss and embroidery needle
* Basic sewing kit
* Sewing machine and matching thread
* Fading fabric marker or water-soluble pen and ruler
* Length of doweling
* Twine, string, or chunky yarn

MAKING THE WALL TIDY

FINISHED SIZE
29 x 21in/74 x 53cm

CUTTING OUT

FROM PATTERNED FABRIC
Cut 1: 6 x16in/15.5 x 41cm rectangle, for top
    pocket
Cut 1: 7½ x 10¾in/19 x 27cm rectangle, for
    bottom pocket
Cut 4: 4½ x 4in/11.5 x 10cm rectangles, for
    appliqué shapes from 2 different patterns

FROM SOLID-COLOR COTTON
Cut 1: 20 x 6in/51 x 15.5cm rectangle, for
    middle pocket
Cut 1: 4¼ x 4¼in/11 x 11cm square, for
    bottom small pocket
Cut 1: 7½ x 4¼in/19 x 11cm rectangle, for
    bottom tall pocket

FROM FELT OR WOOLEN FABRIC
Cut 1: 30 x 21in/76 x 53cm rectangle
NOTE: All measurements include ⅝in/1.5cm
    seam allowance unless otherwise stated.

PREPARING THE POCKETS

1. Machine-sew a length of bias binding to
   the top of all your cut-out pockets. Trim
   any excess at the edges **(A)**.

2. To add the owl and pussycat appliqué,
   copy the cat and owl body templates on
   page 130. Iron fusible web to the wrong
   side of the fabric pieces and cut out the
   shapes. Iron the shapes to the right side
   of two patterned rectangles and secure
   with blanket stitch (see page 11) **(B)**.

A. Adding bias binding to the pocket edges and trimming.

B. Blanket stitching the appliqué shapes in place.

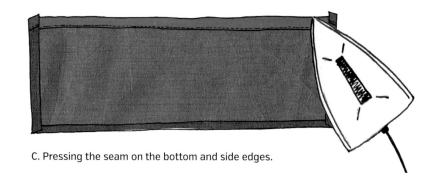

C. Pressing the seam on the bottom and side edges.

3. Press under a ⅝in/1.5cm turning along the bottom of each pocket, and then press a ⅝in/1.5cm turning on the side edges **(C)**. Press under the corners.

SEWING THE POCKETS

4. Pin the pockets in place on the large piece of felt with all the bottom and side edges aligned **(D)**. Machine-sew the pockets in place, just in from the edge around the three sides, remembering to leave the top open!

5. Using a fabric marker pen and ruler, divide the pockets and mark the top and bottom of each dividing line **(E)**. Machine-sew straight lines of stitching, following the marked lines (see tip, below).

D. Positioning the pockets in place on the felt.

FINISHING THE WALL TIDY

6. To make a channel, turn the backing over by 2in/5cm along the top edge and pin. Machine-sew 1½in/3.5cm from the folded edge **(F)**.

7. Push the doweling through the channel. Tie a 24-in/61-cm length of twine or yarn onto the ends of the doweling and your tidy is ready to hang.

E. Marking the pocket divisions.

BETH'S TIP
When sewing the pocket divisions, start from the bottom of the pocket and finish at the top to prevent your fabric puckering.

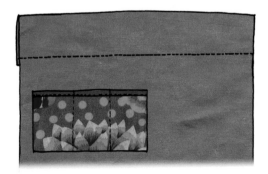

F. Making a channel for the doweling on the top edge.

PERSONALIZED GIFT BAG

This is a sweet little project if you've bought a friend a gift and want to make it really special by giving it to them in a handmade gift bag! You could make it even more personal by putting their name or the date on the front.

THINGS YOU NEED

* Letter or Number templates on pages 132 and 133
* ½yd/½m patterned fabric
* ½yd/½m solid-color cotton fabric, for lining
* Felt
* Iron-on interfacing
* Bias binding
* Embroidery floss and embroidery needle
* Basic sewing kit
* Sewing machine and matching thread

MAKING THE BAG

FINISHED SIZE
Approx 8¾ x 8¾in/22 x 22cm

CUTTING OUT
FROM PATTERNED FABRIC
Cut 2: 9½ x 9in/24 x 23cm rectangles
FROM LINING FABRIC
Cut 2: 9½ x 9in/24 x 23cm rectangles
FROM FELT
8¾x 4in/22 x 10cm, for letters
Cut 4: 13¾ x 1½in/35 x 4cm strips, for handles
NOTE: All measurements include ⅜in/1cm seam
   allowance unless otherwise stated.

PREPARATION
1. Copy the templates for your chosen letters (I used
   "b'day") and cut out from felt, following the tips on
   page 22 for tricky shapes.

2. Cut pieces of interfacing slightly smaller than your
   patterned fabric squares and iron to the wrong side
   of the fabric.

BETH'S TIP
You could use thick wool felt
for the handles, using one
length for each handle rather
than doubling up the pieces.
Attach to the outside of the
bag using a square of running
stitch, with a cross through the
square to reinforce the ends.

SEWING THE LETTERS
3. Pin the letters on the right side of one piece of
   patterned fabric, roughly in the middle. Using a
   contrasting colored embroidery floss and running
   stitch (see page 10), sew the letters in place **(A)**.

A. Sewing the letters to the fabric square.

4. On a flat surface, lay the undecorated patterned
   fabric piece right side up, then the appliquéd piece
   on top, right side down. Next, lay one square of
   lining on top, right side up, followed by the second
   the right side down. Pin all four layers together.

5. Machine-sew all four layers together, taking a
   ⅜in/1cm seam. Sew around three sides leaving the
   top open. Trim the excess fabric and cut the points
   of the corners close to the seam **(B)**. Turn the bag
   right side out.

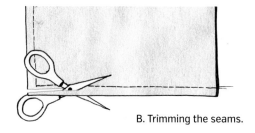

B. Trimming the seams.

MAKING THE BAG

6. Use a length of bias binding (or bind using a length of fabric following the instructions on page 15) to enclose the raw edges on the top of your bag **(C)**.

C. Adding bias binding to the top.

7. Pin two lengths of felt for the handles together, leaving 2½in/6cm at each end unpinned. Pin the open end of the handle length to the bag about 1½in/4cm from the sides, sandwiching the bag between the felt.

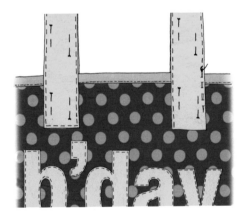

D. Pinning and sewing the handle.

8. Using embroidery floss and running stitch, sew along the length of the handle and across the short end, attaching it to the bag **(D)**.

9. Repeat steps 7 and 8 to add the second handle on the other side of the bag.

PATCHWORK CHAIR PAD

Patchwork is a fabulous way to use up leftover pieces of fabric from other projects. This chair pad cover is straightforward to piece together and will brighten up any tired-looking chair. I bound my chair pad with contrasting bias binding, but you could just stitch the patchwork, batting, and backing together and add ties to the two corners at the back of the chair pad.

THINGS YOU NEED

✣ Patterned fabric in six different patterns, approx ½yd/½m each
✣ Backing fabric, approx ½yd/½m
✣ Sewing machine and matching thread
✣ Batting (wadding), approx ½yd/½m
✣ Basic sewing kit
✣ Fading fabric marker pen
✣ Bias binding, approx 2yd/2¼m

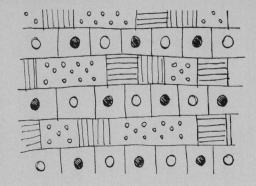

MAKING THE PATCHWORK CHAIR PAD

FINISHED SIZE
12 x 13¾in/30 x 35cm, or to fit your chair

CUTTING OUT
FROM PATTERNED FABRIC
Cut 16: 2½ x 2½in/6.5 x 6.5cm squares
Cut 16: 2½ x7½in/6.5 x 19cm rectangles
NOTE: All measurements include ⅜in/1cm seam
    allowance unless otherwise stated.

PREPARATION
1. Start by choosing the chair you are going to make
    your pad for. Cut a piece of paper roughly the
    shape and size of the chair seat and tape it to the
    chair. Draw around the outside edge of the seat.
    Mark on the template the inside of the chair's back
    struts where the ties will be **(A)**. Cut out following
    the drawn line, adding ⅜in/1cm seam allowance all
    round; to make your template symmetrical, fold it
    in half and trim the edges.

2. Prepare all the squares and rectangles of fabric for
    your patchwork. I used 16 squares and 16 triangles
    from six different fabrics.

MAKING THE PATCHWORK
3. Pin a strip of squares and rectangles together, in
    any order, until you have a strip slightly longer than
    the width of your seat template. Sew each of the
    seams, taking a ⅜in/1cm seam allowance, until
    your strip is complete. Press all seams flat on the
    wrong side. Repeat to make enough strips to cover
    the depth of the seat template **(B)**.

A. Making the chair pad template.

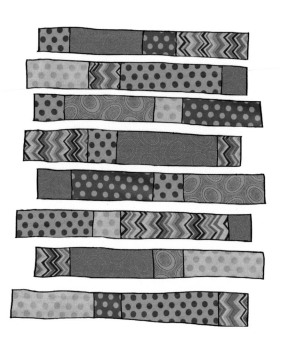

B. Making patchwork strips from squares and rectangles.

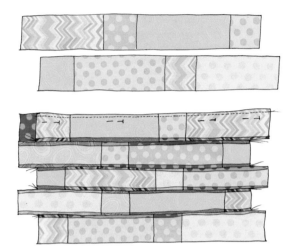

C. Sewing the strips together.

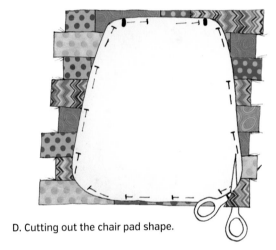

D. Cutting out the chair pad shape.

E. Basting the layers together.

4. Pin the strips right sides facing and sew them together, taking a ⅜in/1cm seam allowance. Press all the long seams open on the wrong side of the pieced patchwork **(C)**.

MAKING THE COVER

5. Pin the seat template to your patchwork piece and cut out **(D)**. Use the template to cut out a piece of backing fabric (marking with a fading fabric marker pen where you need to sew your ties) and a piece of batting.

6. On a flat surface, lay the backing fabric wrong side up, then the batting, then the patchwork piece right side up. Pin the three layers together and then baste using long stitches **(E)**. This will keep all the layers securely together while you sew the binding.

BETH'S TIP
I have chosen six fabrics for my patchwork, as I had quite a lot of leftovers, but you may wish to use as many or as few as you like. Each square and rectangle could be a different fabric, or you could just keep to two or three different patterns. If using a range of different fabrics, work with a limited palette to give a sense of unity to the design. For example, try lots of different prints in toning colors.

7. To make the ties, cut 16in/40cm of binding and machine-sew it together along the open edge. Cut the sewn binding in half and baste the cut ends to the back edge of the chair pad, with raw edges aligned, following the marks you made, with the ties facing inward **(F)**.

BINDING THE COVER

8. Cut 12in/30cm of binding (or a length to match the back edge of your seat). Slip the open edge over the short back edge of the chair pad, enclosing the raw edges and the ends of the ties. Machine-sew in place, just in from the inner folded edge. Trim any excess binding at the ends **(G)**.

9. To bind the chair pad, take a length of binding and machine-sew the first 8in/20cm together (this will make a third tie), then insert the seat pad into the binding and continue to sew as you feed it through the machine **(H)**.

10. Continue around the seat pad to the other side. At the back edge, continue sewing the binding together for 8in/20cm, to make the final tie, before finishing. Trim any excess binding.

F. Attaching the ties.

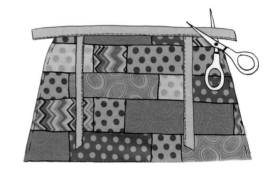

G. Trimming the binding on the back edge.

H. Sewing binding to the chair pad.

PATCHWORK CHAIR PAD

STITCH IT SIMPLE

NORDIC TREE HANGING

This is a really versatile project; once finished you could drape the hanging along a mantelpiece, or make longer lengths and hang them across shelves in your living room or kitchen. Change the motifs to make a pretty year-round hanging—the butterflies on page 32 or the elephants on page 70, would both look really sweet.

THINGS YOU NEED

- Tree templates on page 129
- Patterned fabric
- Felt
- Fabric glue
- Embroidery floss and embroidery needle
- Basic sewing kit
- Batting (wadding)
- Sewing machine and matching thread
- 1¼yd/1½m bias binding

MAKING THE TREE HANGING

FINISHED SIZE
To make 1¼yd/1½m with 7 trees
Trees: Height 5¼in/13.5cm

CUTTING OUT
FROM PATTERNED FABRIC
Cut 14: 5½ x 5½ in/14 x 14cm squares
FROM SCRAPS OF FELT
Cut 7: 5 x 4in/13 x 10cm rectangles
FROM BATTING (WADDING)
Cut 7: 2 x 14in/5 x 35cm rectangles

PREPARATION
1. Copy the tree and tree trunk templates on page 129. Cut four trees from patterned fabric for the front and four from felt for the back. Cut out four tree trunks from felt.

MAKING THE TREES
2. Use a little fabric glue to lightly stick a felt tree trunk to a fabric tree. Using embroidery floss in a contrasting color, running stitch (see page 10) along the tree trunk to secure it to the tree **(A)**.

3. Pin one patterned fabric tree and one felt tree, wrong sides together. Using blanket stitch (see page 11), sew both layers together, starting at the top of the tree. Leave a 2in/5cm gap in the top corner unstitched for stuffing and keep your needle and thread attached **(B)**.

4. Take a length of batting and stuff the tree through the gap. Push the stuffing into all corners of the tree using your fingers or the blunt end of a pencil or knitting needle **(C)**. When your tree is plump, cut off any excess batting.

A. Sewing the trunk in place with running stitch.

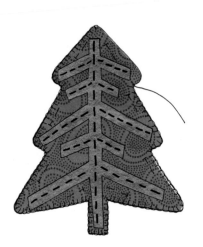

B. Blanket stitching the front and back together.

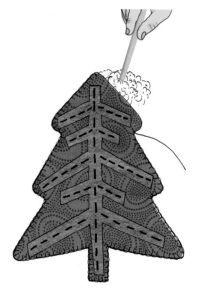

C. Stuffing the tree.

5. Continue with blanket stitch to sew the gap closed. Repeat steps 2–5 to make six more trees.

ATTACHING THE TREES

6. Machine-sew the length of bias binding together to make a hanging strip. Hand-sew each tree to the length of binding, about 8in/20cm apart.

BETH'S TIP
When you stuff your trees with batting, try to use one continuous length to avoid lumps and bumps.

ALTERNATIVE PLACEMAT PROJECT

You could turn the tree design into a festive table center, by sewing the trees to a contrasting solid-color fabric using zig-zag stitch on your machine, appliquéing a circle in the center, and binding the edges with bias binding (see page 15).

TEMPLATES

All the templates are reproduced at 50% of their actual size. Enlarge by 200% on a photocopier or scanner to match the size in the projects.

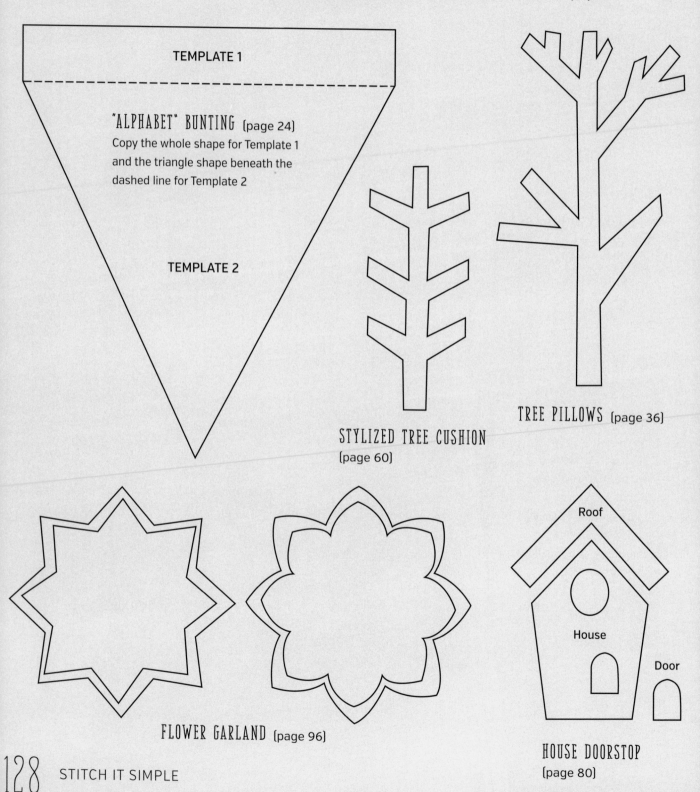

TEMPLATE 1

"ALPHABET" BUNTING [page 24]
Copy the whole shape for Template 1 and the triangle shape beneath the dashed line for Template 2

TEMPLATE 2

STYLIZED TREE CUSHION
[page 60]

TREE PILLOWS [page 36]

FLOWER GARLAND [page 96]

Roof

House

Door

HOUSE DOORSTOP
[page 80]

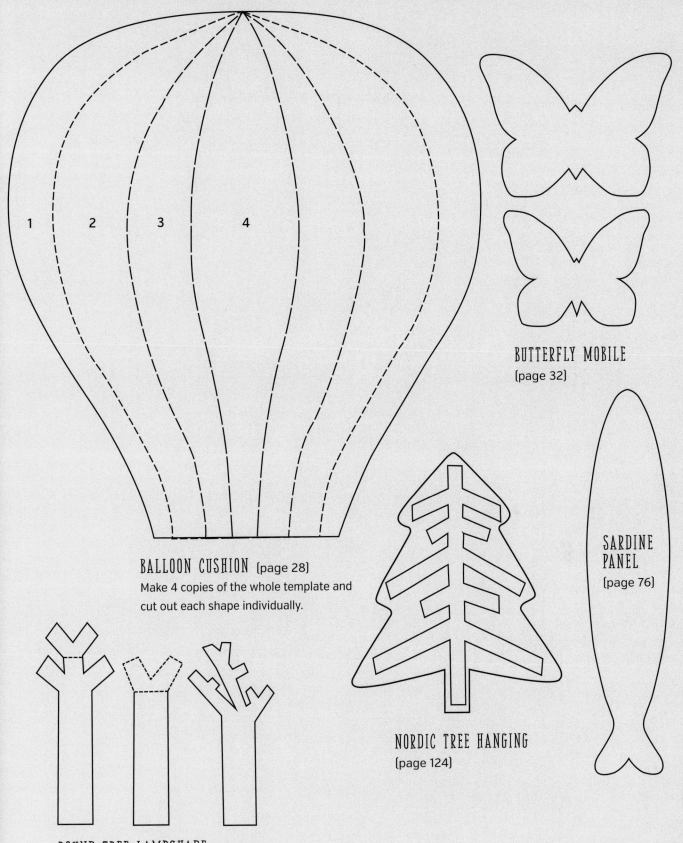

1   2   3   4

BUTTERFLY MOBILE
[page 32]

BALLOON CUSHION [page 28]
Make 4 copies of the whole template and
cut out each shape individually.

SARDINE
PANEL
[page 76]

NORDIC TREE HANGING
[page 124]

ROUND TREE LAMPSHADE [page 16]
Cut along the dashed lines to make variations.

Frosting

Cupcake

CUPCAKE APRON
(page 50)

Liner

PEACOCK TABLE RUNNER
(page 54)

Feather

Wing

Body

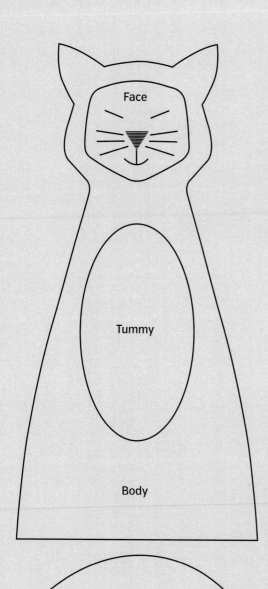

Face

Tummy

Body

Base

KIT AND KAT STUFFED CATS
(page 106)

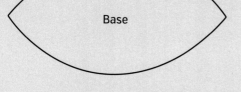

Pussycat

Owl head

Owl body

THE OWL AND THE PUSSYCAT WALL TIDY (page 110)
and BEADY OWL CARD (page 84)

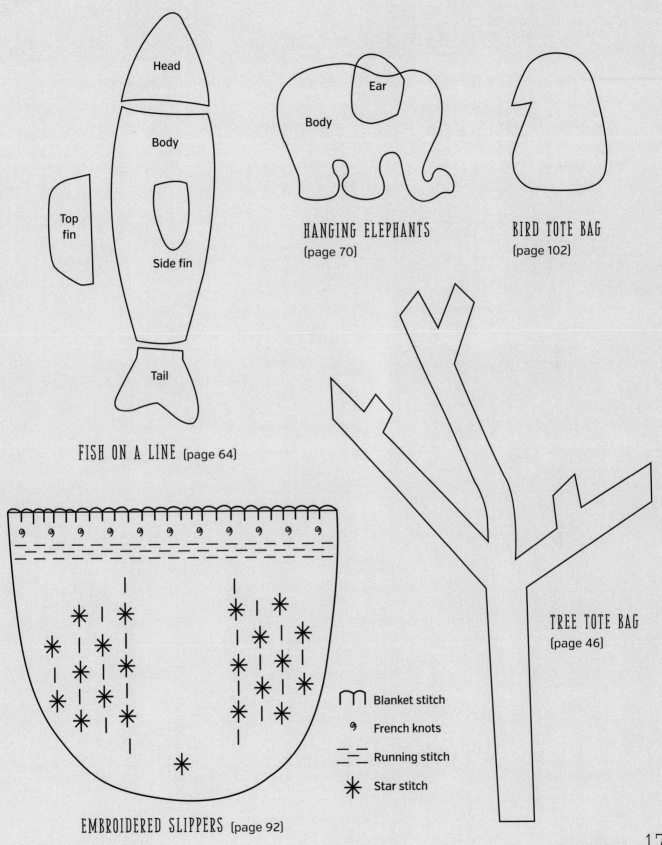

Head

Body

Side fin

Top fin

Tail

FISH ON A LINE (page 64)

Ear

Body

HANGING ELEPHANTS
(page 70)

BIRD TOTE BAG
(page 102)

TREE TOTE BAG
(page 46)

⌐⌐ Blanket stitch

𝕼 French knots

– – Running stitch

✳ Star stitch

EMBROIDERED SLIPPERS (page 92)

Enlarge to match your chosen size for your project.

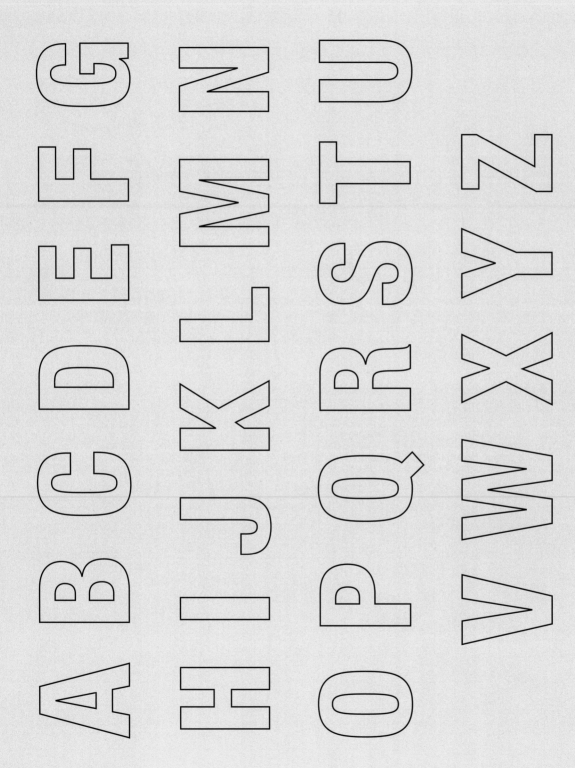

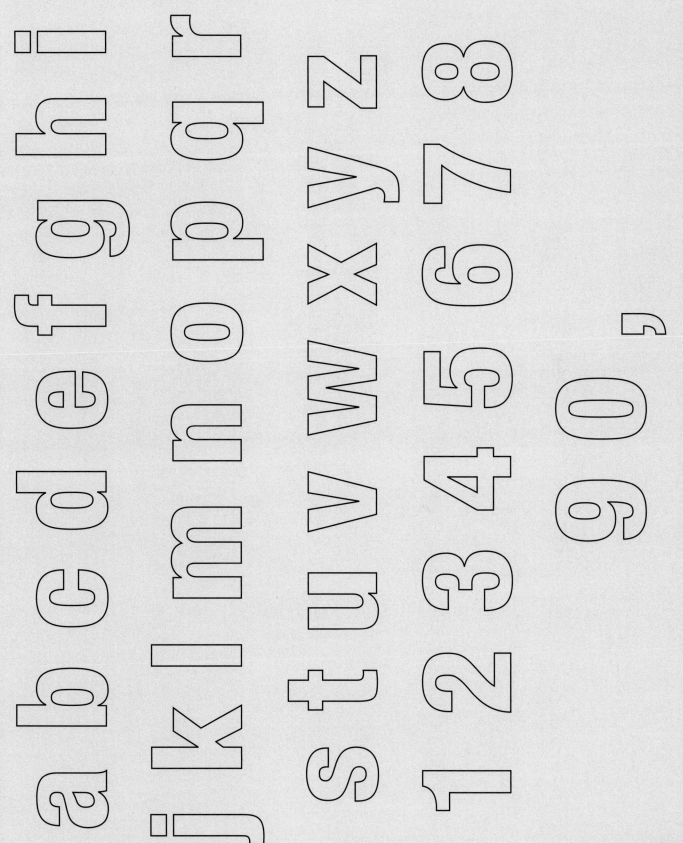

FABRIC LIST

All Rowan fabrics available from Westminster Fibers Inc. (see details on page 136).

ROUND TREE LAMPSHADE   16

GP70 Spot Gold
GP59 Guinea Flower Apricot
GP71 Aboriginal Dot Lime
GP71 Aboriginal Dot Orange
GP20 Paperweight Lime
GP01 Roman Glass Red
Cream canvas/cotton

FABRIC LETTERS   20

GP70 Spot Green
GP70 Spot Red
GP70 Spot Royal
Cream felt

"ALPHABET" BUNTING   24

GP01 Roman Glass Red
GP01 Roman Glass Leafy
BM043 Zigzag Warm
BM015 Rings Grey
BM015 Rings Green
WBROAD Woven Broad Stripe Watermelon
WALTER Woven Alternating Stripe Bliss

BALLOON CUSHION   28

GP70 Spot Sapphire
BM043 Zigzag Multi
GP20 Paperweight Lime
WCATER Woven Caterpillar Stripe Sprout

BUTTERFLY MOBILE   32

GP59 Guinea Flower Apricot
GP59 Guinea Flower Gold
GP59 Guinea Flower Yellow
GP91 Big Blooms Emerald
GP91 Big Blooms Red

TREE PILLOWS   36

GP11 Serape Antique
GP01 Roman Glass Red
BM015 Rings Green

LETTERS AND NUMBERS MINI QUILT   40

BM043 Zigzag Multi
BM043 Zigzag Warm
GP70 Spot Red
GP70 Spot Royal
GP70 Spot Gold
GP70 Spot Fuchsia
GP70 Spot Yellow
GP70 Spot Sapphire
GP70 Spot Green

TREE TOTE BAG   46

GP59 Guinea Flower Apricot
SC035 Shot Cotton Sunshine
GP01 Roman Glass Red
GP01 Roman Glass Leafy

CUPCAKE APRON   50

GP71 Aboriginal Dot Terracotta

PEACOCK TABLE RUNNER   54

BM043 Zigzag Warm
GP01 Roman Glass Red
GP59 Guinea Flower Gold
SC35 Shot Cotton Sunshine
SC90 Shot Cotton Eucalyptus

STYLIZED TREE CUSHION   60

SC07 Shot Cotton Persimmon
GP01 Roman Glass Red
GP01 Roman Glass Purple
GP20 Paperweight Lime

FISH ON A LINE   64

GP70 Spot Yellow
GP70 Spot Teal
SC35 Shot Cotton Sunshine
SC90 Shot Cotton Eucalyptus

Cream felt
Green felt

HANGING ELEPHANTS   70
GP71 Aboriginal Dot Ocean
GP71 Aboriginal Dot Terracotta
Yellow felt
Green felt

SARDINE PANEL   76
SC90 Shot Cotton Eucalyptus
GP117 Ombre Pink
GP117 Ombre Red
GP117 Ombre Brown

HOUSE DOORSTOP   80
Cream felt
Green felt
Orange felt

BEADY OWL CARD   84
SC90 Shot Cotton Eucalyptus
BM043 Zigzag Warm
GP70 Spot Sapphire
GP70 Spot Gold

CIRCLES CUSHION   88
SC35 Shot Cotton Sunshine
GP117 Ombre Pink
GP71 Aboriginal Dot Terracotta
GP71 Aboriginal Dot Ocean
GP71 Aboriginal Dot Leaf

EMBROIDERED SLIPPERS   92
Red felt

FLOWER GARLAND   96
GP59 Guinea Flower Apricot
GP59 Guinea Flower Gold
GP59 Guinea Flower Yellow
GP91 Big Blooms Emerald
GP91 Big Blooms Red

BIRD TOTE BAG   102
SC35 Shot Cotton Sunshine
SC90 Shot Cotton Eucalyptus
SC07 Shot Cotton Persimmon
SC91 Shot Cotton Pea Soup
GP59 Guinea Flower Apricot
GP20 Paperweight Lime

KIT AND KAT STUFFED CATS   106
GP20 Paperweight Lime
GP01 Roman Glass Red
Cream Felt

THE OWL AND THE PUSSYCAT WALL TIDY   110
SC91 Shot Cotton Pea Soup
GP91 Big Blooms Red
GP91 Big Blooms Emerald
Red felt

PERSONALIZED GIFT BAG   114
GP70 Spot Sapphire
GP70 Spot Red
Yellow felt

PATCHWORK CHAIR PAD   118
GP70 Spot Yellow
GP70 Spot Sapphire
GP70 Spot Green
BM043 Zigzag Warm
GP71 Aboriginal Dot Ocean
GP71 Aboriginal Dot Leaf

NORDIC TREE HANGING   124
GP71 Aboriginal Dot Leaf
GP71 Aboriginal Dot Terracotta
Red felt
Green felt

STOCKISTS

FABRICS AND NOTIONS

USA
Westminster Fibers, Inc.
www.westminster fibers.com

Coats & Clark
www.makeitcoats.com

Felt Craft
www.feltcraft.com

UK
Coats Crafts UK
www.makeitcoats.com

John Lewis plc
www.johnlewis.com

Wool Felt Company
www.woolfeltcompnay.co.uk

LAMPSHADE KITS, BAGS, APRONS

USA
www.ebay.com
www.etsy.com
www.universal-textiles.com

UK
www.ebay.co.uk
www.etsy.com/uk
www.needcraft.co.uk
www.universal-textiles.com/uk-ut

ACKNOWLEDGMENTS

AUTHOR'S ACKNOWLEDGMENTS

This being my first book, I truly had no idea of the sheer amount of time and work that would go into putting a book together, so a huge thanks go out to everyone who contributed: friends, family, and colleagues through their encouragement, advice, support and for putting up with me talking about this project for over a year.

A special thank you to the following people: Steve for his fantastic photography, and Katie and Anne, for sticking with me through all the edits, changes, more edits and amendments, and for making the book look and read better than I could have imagined.

Kaffe and Brandon, for taking a chance on me and allowing me to be part of your inspirational world... and of course for your beautiful fabrics.

Ben, for always believing in me and giving me the best motivational pep talks–your unwaivering support and love has kept me going. My amazing Mum and Dad for supporting me in whatever it is I do, for your meticulous proofreading and feedback, and your sound guidance, always.

Louie, for getting *Stitch it Simple* out in the world.

And especially thank you to Susan–this book would not exist without you, so my sincere thanks for all your time, patience, guidance, skill, and expertise in making *Stitch it Simple* happen.

This book is dedicated to my gran, Lilian, who could sew better with her eyes closed than I will ever be able to, and to Si, Es, and my beautiful niece, Alice–you unknowingly inspired so many projects in this book, so this is for you.

PUBLISHERS' ACKNOWLEDGMENTS

The publishers would like to thank Kaffe Fassett for his foreword, Steve, Beth, Anne, and Katie for their excellent work on photography, illustrations, layouts, and text respectively, and JJ Locations and Sarah Tolner for providing the venues for photography.